CEO Guide to Doing Business in New Zealand

By Ade Asefeso MCIPS MBA

ISBN 978-1-291-66380-8

Publisher: AA Global Sourcing Ltd
Website: http://www.aaglobalsourcing.com

Table of Contents

Disclaimer

Dedication

This book is dedicated to my family and friends who seems to have been sent here to teach me something about who I am supposed to be. They have nurtured me, challenged me, and even opposed me…. But at every juncture has taught me!

This book is dedicated to my lovely boys, Thomas, Michael and Karl. Teaching them to manage their finance will give them the lives they deserve. They have taught me more about life, presence, and energy management than anything I have done in my life.

Chapter 1: Introduction

New Zealand is a relatively easy country in which to conduct business due to a number of historical and business environment similarities it shares with the United Kingdom. New Zealand enjoys a long history of association with the UK and today the UK is New Zealand's sixth-largest trading partner.

New Zealand has a modern, prosperous and developed economy. With a small and sophisticated market New Zealand provides many opportunities for UK, EU and American companies both experienced in and new to exporting.

New Zealand's lifestyle is often called relaxed with a moderate climate, open environment, reasonable public services, and relative security from war and terrorism. In general New Zealanders enjoy a comfortable standard of living.

New Zealand's economy is closely tied to Australia's, and both held up better than most during the global financial crisis. The downside to the resilience of its economy is that the New Zealand dollar has appreciated, making the country's agricultural exports more expensive. The higher prices have helped to push up unemployment to 7.3% the highest level since 1999.

New Zealand is physically remote; two specks of green in the vast Pacific Ocean and 1,500 km away from its nearest neighbour, Australia. Despite this physical remoteness, New Zealand is a sophisticated country, deeply engaged with the rest of the world economically, culturally and through a myriad of personal connections.

New Zealand population is small, just over four million, but is ethnically diverse as New Zealand is a nation of migrants. The statistics tell the story. One in every four people now working in New Zealand was born elsewhere while one New Zealander in four is currently living and working overseas.

New Zealand enjoys a stable democracy with a proportional representation voting system which tends to produce coalition governments. New Zealand was rated first or first equal for freedom from corruption by Transparency International's Corruption Barometer in each of the last five years.

New Zealand stock exchange is the first in the world to open trading each day as its time zone (in GMT) puts New Zealand two hours ahead of Sydney, three hours ahead of Tokyo, four hours ahead of Singapore, 12 hours ahead of London and 17 hours ahead of New York.

New Zealand culture assigns a high value to fairness, ingenuity, practicality, modesty, restraint and informality. These values have remained remarkably consistent over time, surviving radical changes to the country's social and economic fabric.

The pattern of economic change in New Zealand over the past 40 years has been driven by three core principles: diversification, liberalisation and transparency.

Diversification

When New Zealand was Britain's farm and could make a good living by selling sheep carcasses, cheese and butter to the British market, life was fairly uncomplicated. New Zealand export earnings were so strong that they were able to insulate the domestic economy from marketplace realities through widespread use of subsidies and import controls to shelter a manufacturing sector, much of which was either inefficient or only marginally efficient.

When Britain joined the European Economic Community in 1973, however, all of that became unsustainable. New Zealand had no choice but to diversify both its products and markets. The adjustment process was initially slow and difficult but New Zealand now exports throughout the Asia-Pacific region as well as to North America, the Middle East and Europe. Dairy and meat are still significant contributors to overall GDP but tourism now rivals pastoral agriculture as a leading export earner. New Zealand also has developing industries in export education, boat building, IT, horticulture, wine and film.

Liberalisation

The loss of the preferential trade relationship with Britain and the need to compete for export sales with lower cost countries forced a radical re-engineering of New Zealand's economic policies. As a result, New Zealand now has one of the most open economies in the world and is ranked first of 181 countries in the latest World Bank Doing Business survey for ease of starting a new business and third for ease of doing business.

Moves to deregulate the economy have included floating the New Zealand dollar, privatising or corporatising many State-Owned Enterprises, deregulating the labour market and dismantling protectionism. The policy preference of both major political parties; National and Labour is to rely on market disciplines except where those disciplines are blunted by market dominance (as in competition law) or where the political judgement is that they might deliver outcomes which are socially unacceptable (occupational health and safety, the statutory minimum wage).

Those tariffs which remain are few by comparison with almost all other countries, and low. New Zealand is also party to a number of free trade agreements, including with China and Australia. The agreement with Australia has created a trans-Tasman marketplace for most goods and services and significant harmonisation of regulatory requirements.

Few restrictions are imposed on businesses establishing in New Zealand, with freedom of choice extending to the type of business, its size and its location. Capital is allowed to flow freely both inwards and outwards.

Transparency

Transparency and clear accountability are key features of New Zealand's public sector and institutional framework.

The Reserve Bank Act 1989 makes the Reserve Bank independent from Government and tasks it with keeping future price inflation between 1% and 3% on average over the medium term. There is, however, flexibility within the Act for the Reserve Bank to "look through" one-off price shocks in order to avoid unnecessary instability in output, interest rates and the exchange rate.

The Fiscal Responsibility Act 1994 requires the Government to set explicit fiscal objectives and to specify its intentions for fiscal management beyond the next 12 months. It also commits the Treasury to produce regular updates through the year on the fiscal and economic position. The idea is to encourage fiscal discipline.

Legal system

New Zealand's common law system is similar to that in England and many other western countries, and has familiarity with most international legal structures especially in the finance and corporate law areas.

New Zealand has a hierarchy of generalist courts; the District Court, the High Court, the Court of Appeal and the Supreme Court. Most criminal and civil matters are dealt with by the District Court with the High Court handling the larger and most serious cases. A right of appeal exists from the High Court to the Court of Appeal and, with leave, to the Supreme Court.

New Zealand has a single legal profession in which most members hold a practising certificate as barrister and solicitor. Judges are appointed by the Governor-General on the advice of the Attorney-General and there is a strong tradition of judicial independence.

Chapter 2: Strengths of the Market

In brief these are:

1. Similar legal and financial systems to those in the UK.
2. Strong historical ties with anecdotally around 70% of the New Zealand population claiming links back to the UK.
3. Best placed to supply Pacific Islands.
4. A perfectly sized market for UK, EU and US Small to Medium Enterprise (SME) new to exporting.
5. The least corrupt country in which to do business (2013 Corruptions Perception Index).
6. English speaking.
7. Many of the population travel widely; young New Zealanders continue to travel the world often using the UK as a base during their Overseas Experience holiday,
8. Free Trade Agreements with countries including Australia (CER), China (NZ-China FTA), Singapore (NZSCEP), Thailand (NZTCEP), and New Zealand-Hong Kong, China (CEP),
9. The New Zealand government continues to extend its reach into the wider global trading community with trade agreements currently under negotiation including Russia, Belarus and Kazakhstan (NZ-RBK), India (NZ-India FTA), and Korea (NZ-Korea FTA).

Opportunities in New Zealand

New Zealand's small market size has many opportunities to offer UK, EU and American companies. Its size in particular makes the market a sound choice for UK, EU and American SME companies new to exporting and whose manufacturing capacity suits the smaller market.

The value of the US and UK's reputation in making high-quality goods should not be forgotten in this region where high quality can compete successfully with lower priced (and lower quality) goods sourced from other countries.

New Zealand imports a wide range of British and American goods and services, particularly in the following sectors:

- Agriculture
- Biotechnology
- Clothing
- Creative Industries
- Education
- Food and Drink
- Giftware
- Healthcare & Pharmaceuticals
- ICT
- Marine
- Publishing
- Textiles

UK, EU and American goods and services can also find a place in the New Zealand market in many other sectors such as Aerospace, Automotive, Engineering, and Footwear. In general if the product is good and suits the local market then there is every chance it will sell in New Zealand.

UK exports to New Zealand were worth £507m in the 12 months end January 2012. The January 2012 to July 2012 period saw

£304m worth of goods exported from the UK to New Zealand (an increase of 14%).

Top 10 exports from the UK are from the automotive, machinery and mechanical appliances, printing, pharmaceutical, food and beverage, optical medical and measuring equipment, and electrical machinery and equipment sectors.

New Zealand's top 10 imports of main commodities from all countries are:
1. Petroleum and products.
2. Mechanical machinery and equipment.
3. Vehicles, parts, and accessories.
4. Electrical machinery and equipment.
5. Textiles and textile articles.
6. Aircraft and parts included in this list due to one-off importation of large aircraft.
7. Plastic and plastic articles.
8. Optical, medical, and measuring equipment.
9. Iron and steel, and articles.
10. Pharmaceutical products.
11. Paper and paperboard, and articles.

Note: The one-off importation of large aircraft had a large influence on the import value. Aircraft imports were part of Air New Zealand's fleet upgrade.

As at August 2012 top imports by country of origin are People's Republic of China, Australia, United States of America, Japan, Singapore, Germany, Republic of Korea, Malaysia, Thailand and the United Kingdom.

Chapter 3: Economic Overview

New Zealand has a mixed economy which operates on free market principles. It has sizeable manufacturing and service sectors complementing a highly efficient agricultural sector. Exports of goods and services account for around one third of real expenditure GDP.

Over the last quarter of a century, the New Zealand economy has changed from being one of the most regulated in the Organisation for Economic Cooperation and Development (OECD) to one of the least regulated.

1. Economic activity as measured by GDP increased 0.6 percent in the June 2012 quarter.
2. Economic activity for the year end June 2012 was up 2.0 percent.

Other statistics as listed on the Statistics New Zealand website are: Gross domestic product (GDP):

3. Agriculture (up 4.7 percent) was the largest contributor to economic growth in the June 2012 quarter.
4. Construction (up 3.3 percent) and manufacturing (up 0.8 percent) also increased.
5. On the expenditure measure of GDP:
6. The expenditure measure of GDP was up 0.3 percent in the June 2012 quarter.
7. The volume of expenditure by New Zealand households was up 0.2 percent.
8. For the year end June 2012, expenditure on GDP was up 1.7 percent.

Economic Recovery

Following the Global Financial Crisis, New Zealand's own recession in 2008, and the Christchurch earthquakes, New Zealand has been experiencing a gradual recovery. GDP is forecast to increase to above 3 percent.

Renewed optimism in the economy drove consumer and business confidence upwards. The main supports to economic growth include low interest rates, strong growth in New Zealand's largest trading partners (China and Australia), and the Christchurch rebuild.

The Canterbury Rebuild

A powerful earthquake on the 22nd of February 2011 devastated the Christchurch central business area as well as a number of suburbs resulting in severe structural damage to buildings, infrastructure and fatalities.

The New Zealand economy had held up relatively well to recent recessionary forces but the February Christchurch earthquake led to a damage estimate of NZ$20 billion (10% of GDP) much of which is covered by private insurance, which is reinsured through overseas insurance companies, and the government-owned Earthquake Commission.

The Canterbury rebuild is expected to be a significant driver of economic growth over the next five to ten years. Ongoing after-shocks continue delaying some aspects of the rebuild. Many businesses relocated and were able to remain trading. Opportunities for UK, EU and American companies exist in rebuilding infrastructure.

Chapter 4: Business Overview

Getting Your Goods to the Market

Customers in New Zealand will expect products and services to be delivered on time. The main delivery options for New Zealand are sea freight, airfreight, post, air parcel post, and express or courier service. The best delivery method depends on speed, cost, reliability and product requirement (e.g. fragile or hanging garments). For all methods, except post, it is often easier to use a freight forwarder. Forwarders should be approached in the early stages of market research rather than waiting until the goods are ready to go.

Standards and Technical Regulation

Standards New Zealand is the trading arm of the Standards Council; a crown entity operating under the Standards Act 1988. The Standards Council, an appointed body with representatives from all sectors of the community, oversees the development and adoption of Standards and standards-related products. The information centre can provide standards information that ranges from the availability and price of a standard to complex research into technical requirements for export markets.

Business Etiquette, Language and Culture

Around 70% of New Zealanders claim at least some British Ancestry and British and American visitors will usually feel quite at home. New Zealanders tend towards informality; visitors may soon find themselves addressed by their Christian or first names.

Internet/email

Due to New Zealand's isolated geographical location and time difference with the rest of the world e-mail, e-commerce and the internet are all playing a major part in the way New Zealanders do business. UK, EU and American companies visiting New Zealand should have an e-mail address on their business cards. New Zealand companies will expect prompt responses to email communications.

Per capita, New Zealand is one of the most Internet connected nations in the world and most New Zealand companies now have their own website. Business is likely to be done by email rather than fax. All hotels provide internet link facilities and there are numerous cyber cafes in the larger towns and cities.

Social media

The use of Twitter, LinkedIn and Facebook is growing fast as marketing and communications tools for businesses.

Getting Paid - Terms of Payment

Generally speaking, any of the customary methods of payment used in international commercial transactions can be used when doing business with New Zealand companies. Companies should contact an international branch of their own bank to advise the best route for their money to be transferred to the UK, EU and USA. Banks can also give advice on credit management and short-term credit insurance and factoring.

How to Invest in New Zealand

New Zealand's efficient, market-driven economy delivers key benefits to investors, including business stability, extensive free-trade agreements, and active government support for investment.
New Zealand is an export nation connected locally and globally by efficient technology and logistics. New Zealand has fast digital and wireless networks. New Zealand has efficient ports, a wide range of global airline services, and high-capacity submarine fibre-optic cables.

New Zealand's business-friendly taxation system supports capital development, research and development and international investment. Flexible labour policies ensure low employee add-on costs and minimal losses of work days to industrial action. New Zealand's competitive property and telecommunications costs also attract multinational investment projects to New Zealand.

Chapter 5: Preparing to Export to New Zealand

Despite the relative ease with which business can be conducted in New Zealand it is important to fully prepare before arriving in New Zealand. Market research is vital to success.

As stated before in this book New Zealand is one of the least corrupt countries and as such is a relatively easy country to do business with. New Zealand's closeness in terms of distance and free trade agreements with Australia and Asian countries makes New Zealand companies well-versed in the business of importing and exporting.

EU, US and UK companies should note that many New Zealand firms rank at the top in some specialist sectors (for example Weta Workshop for their work on animation in films such as the Lord of the Rings Trilogy). New Zealand is a modern sophisticated country.

Key areas for business

With a third of New Zealand's national population (around 1.5 million) living in the Auckland region this must be seen as one of the key areas for business. It is the largest industrial and commercial centre, with a major port and the main international airport in New Zealand.

Wellington is the capital city. It is the seat of government, and a major port (population around 448,000). Christchurch (population around 521,000) is the major centre of the South Island served by an international airport and the large port of Lyttelton. The city has an increasing output in science and technology and is an important agricultural, industrial and trading centre.

Other cities include Hamilton, Tauranga, New Plymouth, Dunedin and Invercargill.

Representatives in the market

New Zealand importers, exposed to international competition and the proximity of the Asian market, have become experienced world traders, keenly aware of prices and margins. Direct importing by retailers occurs more frequently with the resulting demise of many traditional middlemen.

Three main distribution options for UK, EU and American exporters are:
1. Appoint a wholesaler
2. Sell direct to importing retailers
3. Appoint sales agents and sub-contract logistics functions to third parties.

Most New Zealand importers travel regularly to the major international trade fairs and are therefore well aware of new trends and opportunities. Internet, email and increasingly e-commerce are the norm in New Zealand business.

Most New Zealand agents or distributors will want to operate on an exclusive basis due to the relatively small size of the market. It is important to offer support to any agent or distributor through regular correspondence and visits. It is advisable to offer support for marketing either in the form of finance or by providing point of sale and marketing merchandise.

It is generally advised not to appoint an agent in Australia to look after New Zealand unless the importer has a good presence in both countries with an adequate branch structure. Importers tend to concentrate on their home markets. Although the economies of both countries are becoming increasingly integrated they are not a single market. Some New Zealand importers also market into the Pacific Islands and the potential in these countries should be noted.

Import controls

There are no import licence requirements (removed in July 1992) or quotas in New Zealand. All imports require customs clearance once they cross the border. They are generally processed by a nominated Customs Broker.

Import duty concessions are usually granted when there are no suitable alternatives from New Zealand manufacturers and are usually available for use by all importers. Applications can be made to NZ Customs for interpretations of concessions. (Cost approx. NZ$40). If a concession is possible (and is not already in place) it can be applied for through the Ministry of Economic Development www.med.govt.nz (cost approx. NZ$200.)

Additional taxes

All goods imported into New Zealand for business or commercial purposes are liable for Customs duty and other applicable fees. Charges are calculated using the following:
1. The Customs value of the goods; usually the transaction value (the purchase price for the goods).

2. Customs duty; tariff classification and duty rate applied to each good which comes from the Working Tariff Document of New Zealand.
3. Concession.
4. Preferential tariff.
5. Goods and services tax (GST) calculated on the total of the value of the goods plus the duty plus any freight and insurance charges.

Also where applicable the following fees and charges will be collected:
6. Import entry transaction fee.
7. Inward cargo transaction fee.
8. Ministry of Agriculture and Forestry bio-security system entry levy.
9. Anti-dumping and countervailing duties
10. Alcoholic and Liquor Advisory Council (ALAC) levy.
11. Heavy Engineering Research Association (HERA) levy.

Goods and Services Tax (GST)

GST is an indirect tax that is imposed on each sale or supply of goods and services starting from production and ending with the sale to the final consumer. Intermediate suppliers of goods and services receive a credit for GST paid so that the cost of the GST is borne only by the final consumer. Goods and Services Tax (GST) is 15 percent.

Import Entry Transaction Fee

An Import Entry Transaction Fee of NZ$38.07 (GST inclusive) is payable on every import entry clearance and import declaration for goods. The fee includes the Ministry for Primary Industries bio-security system entry levy of NZ$12.77 (GST inclusive).

The total, NZ$38.07, is collected at the same time as duty and/or GST. This is charged and shown separately on Deferred Payment and Cash Statements. The fee is included with the Duty and GST amount shown on the "Cleared Entry Message" received by importers and Customs Brokers who lodge electronic import entries.

Chapter 6: Legislation and Local Regulations

All legislation relating to the conduct of business and the operation of companies in New Zealand is enacted by New Zealand's parliament and administered by New Zealand government agencies. The Commerce Act 1986 provides the framework for promoting competition in markets for the long-term benefit of consumers. There are no import licence requirements or quotas in New Zealand. All imports require customs clearance once they cross the border.

Controls on Trading

The Commerce Act 1986 and the Fair Trading Act 1986 are New Zealand's competition laws, aimed at protecting the competitive practice. Acts can be viewed at www.legislation.govt.nz

1. The Commerce Act 1986

The Commerce Act prohibits anti-competitive collusive and unilateral behaviour, and mergers that create or strengthen a dominant position in the market. The Commerce Commission is the public enforcement agency.

2. Fair Trading Act, 1996

This Act consolidates the law on misleading advertising: prohibits deceptive or misleading conduct and false representations about the provision of goods and services, prohibits certain unfair trading practices and provides for new consumer information and product safety standards. Enforcement is undertaken by the Commerce Commission.

3.   Consumer Guarantees Act, 1993

The Act, administered by the Ministry of Consumer Affairs www.consumer-ministry.govt.nz creates statutory guarantees, which are given automatically every time a trader supplies goods or services to a consumer. This includes all items bought for everyday use.

It includes regulations that manufacturers/importers must ensure that all goods are of acceptable quality i.e. they must be free from minor faults, they must be safe and durable and the goods must correspond with any description, sample or demonstration model which is given to the consumer. In addition the law enforces that consumers should pay no more than a reasonable price unless a price has been agreed.

The Ministry of Consumer Affairs Trading Standards Service has a consumer safety function; they educate consumers and traders in identifying safe products and using them safely. The Ministry can suggest modifications to make a product safe, request that unsafe products be removed from sale, assist companies recall unsafe products and help develop voluntary standards.

Parallel Importing

Since May 1998, an amendment to the Copyright Act has permitted the parallel importation of products subject to copyright (with the exception of medicines). This means that, providing a product was lawfully made, anybody may import it into New Zealand, with or without the permission of the copyright owner, and notwithstanding any exclusive distribution agreements the copyright owner may have entered into with other parties.

While there has been no discernible change in consumer buying habits, and nobody has yet established dedicated ongoing lines of supply to bypass authorised suppliers, the ability for this to occur in the future has implications for British, European and American traders looking to appoint agents (and those renegotiating existing agency agreements) in New Zealand.

Responding to Tenders

Tenders can be found on various websites such as GETS (www.gets.govt.nz), LGTenders (www.lgtenders.co.nz), and Tenderlink (www.tenderlink.com). As with all business communication with New Zealand companies responses are expected on time. UK, EU and American companies should look carefully at tender documentation and follow rules pertaining to each tender. New Zealand has zero corruption so bribes are not the norm in New Zealand.

Tenders issued by the New Zealand Government can be accessed via the New Zealand Government Electronic Tenders Services website www.gets.govt.nz. Registration is required and is a fast and easy process. Note some tenders on this site tend to have relatively short time-frames and a UK, EU and American company will find strong competition from local companies who may already have inside information about new tenders.

Recruiting and Retaining Staffing

New Zealand's deregulated labour market is based on voluntary union membership, individual employment contracts, and proactive recruitment of skilled overseas workers. It has a highly educated and multi-skilled workforce. New Zealanders are famed for their "can do" and "Kiwi know-how" attitude.

In the June 2012 quarter compared with the March 2012 quarter statistics released by Statistics New Zealand in the Household Labour Force Survey list:

1. The employment rate fell 0.3 percentage points to 63.8 percent
2. The number of people employed decreased by 2,000 people
3. The unemployment rate rose 0.1 percentage point to 6.8 percent
4. The number of people unemployed increased by 2,000
5. The labour force participation rate fell from 68.7 percent to 68.4 percent.

The employment of staff is done so in accordance with the Employment Relations Act 2000. A key principle of this act is that parties to employment relationships must deal with each other in good faith.

Labelling and Packaging Regulations

Labelling and packaging regulations in New Zealand vary depending on the type of product being sold. As a general rule, UK, EU and American suppliers would be well advised to label their goods "Made in UK", "Made in USA", etc. Such indications have a much greater attraction in New Zealand where there is a traditional preference for goods made in the UK and US. For some products, such as clothing and footwear, country of origin labelling is compulsory.

Information on fibre content labelling, care labelling and country of origin labelling for clothing and textiles can be found on New Zealand's Commerce Commission website www.comcom.govt.nz. Packaging and labelling requirements for food and beverages are outlined on the Ministry for Primary Industries website www.foodsafety.govt.nz.

Chapter 7: Getting There

Passports/visas

All visitors must have a valid passport, including return tickets. British passport holders can enter New Zealand as a visitor for up to six months on arrival without a visa, provided they can satisfy an Immigration Officer that they meet the requirements of the rules. Anyone wishing to work in New Zealand requires a work visa.

Health advice

New Zealand is considered one of the healthiest countries in the world in which to travel and no special health precautions are necessary.

1. All local water supplies are drinkable and food supplies meet strict New Zealand government regulations. Bottled water is available from supermarkets and retail stores.
2. New Zealand has no vaccination requirements; however the World Health Organisation recommends that all travellers should be covered for diphtheria, tetanus, measles, mumps, rubella, chicken pox, polio and Hepatitis B regardless of their destination.
3. Special care should be taken in exposure to the sun. The ozone layer over New Zealand is thinner than elsewhere and burn times are much shorter than the UK and US.
4. Research has shown that asthma sufferers may be more at risk of an attack in New Zealand and sufferers should be suitably prepared.
5. Outbreaks of avian influenza ('bird flu') in Asia and Europe have heightened international health agencies' concern about

the possibility of an influenza pandemic occurring. There are no recorded cases of bird flu in New Zealand.

There is a limited arrangement with New Zealand covering emergency medical treatment; visitors are, however, strongly advised to take out comprehensive medical insurance to cover treatment outside this arrangement.

Travelling to New Zealand by Air

New Zealand is well served by daily flights from the UK. Flight times vary between 23 and 27 hours. Twenty foreign airlines operate aircraft in New Zealand with a further nineteen international airlines operating on a code-share only basis to New Zealand.

From 1 July 2008 international passengers are no longer required to pay a departure fee. A Passenger Services Charge (PSC) is levied on airlines.

Travel times by air:
- Auckland-Wellington 1 hour
- Auckland-Christchurch 1 hour 30 minutes
- Auckland-Sydney 3 hours 20 minutes

Rail

New Zealand has a limited railway network with reasonable train travel and the trains modern and comfortable. KiwiRail Scenic Journeys run three core services; the Northern Explorer runs from Auckland to Wellington, the Coastal Pacific from Picton to Christchurch, and the TranzAlpine from Christchurch to Greymouth.

Roads

There are over 96,000 km of roads, over 11,000 km of which are State highways. Traffic travels on the left side of the road with a speed limit of 100km/h on the open road and 50km/h in residential areas.

Greater Auckland is spread out over a wide area with many industrial and commercial centres several miles out from the city centre. Because public transport is not well developed for these districts, and taxis can be fairly expensive, many visitors prefer to make use of hire cars.

Car Hire

Self-drive cars are available in the main towns. Hire is by day or week. Visitors will be required to produce a valid driving licence before they can take delivery of a hire car. British and American driving licences are accepted for this purpose. Arrangements can be made with hire firms where a car hired in one town can be surrendered in another, usually at no extra cost.

Taxis

Taxis are available in nearly all cities and towns in New Zealand. The NZ Taxi Federation has a list of all federation approved service providers.

Buses

Good bus services operate in most of the larger towns of New Zealand. InterCity Coachlines is the main operator for long distance travel.

Getting to and from the Airport

All airports are well served by shuttle buses and taxis. Auckland airport is 8km from Wellington and Christchurch 12km.

Hotels

New Zealand has a wide range of modern hotels and motels throughout the country. Tariffs vary significantly depending on the hotel, season and the locality. When making bookings it is worth enquiring about any business or corporate rates. Detailed information about accommodation can be obtained from Tourism New Zealand.

Restaurants

In addition to the restaurants in the hotels, there are good restaurants in all main towns. Usual liquor licensing hours in hotels are from 11am to 11pm. Most hotels have later hours on Friday and Saturday evenings. Licensed restaurants may serve liquor to diners from noon one day to 1.00 am on the following day. A number of unlicensed restaurants have permits whereby patrons may bring their own liquor (BYO) and some are both licensed and BYO.

Tipping

In general, tipping is not a common practice in New Zealand. In some high-tourist destinations such as Rotorua and Queenstown the practice is becoming accepted. The decision lies in the hand of the visitor.

Electricity

The electricity supply is 230/250 volts AC, 50 cycles. Plug fittings are all of a three flat pin type which are not used in Europe. Plug conversion sockets are widely available. Most hotels, motels etc have razor points. Bayonet lamp fittings are widely used.

Chapter 8: New Zealand Immigration Policy

New Zealand has a reasonably open door immigration policy, particularly for skilled migrants and for entrepreneurs with the resources and capital to contribute to the economy by setting up a business in New Zealand.

If you are not a New Zealand or an Australian national, you will need a visa to work in New Zealand.

Visa types include:
1. Temporary work visa
2. Highly skilled visa
3. Long-term business visa, and
4. Residence visa.

Applicants for any visa must:
1. Be of good character, and
2. Hold a valid passport which expires later than three months after the proposed date of departure.

Work visa

Work visas are time-limited and can be issued for a period of up to three years. To qualify foreign nationals must have a job offer:
1. For an occupation on the skills shortage list, or

From a New Zealand employer who:
2. Is accredited or has approval to recruit foreign workers, or
3. Can prove there are no suitable New Zealand applicants for the job.

An applicant may also be eligible when going to New Zealand for a specific purpose which will be of benefit to New Zealand.

Employees of a business which is relocating to New Zealand can also apply for a work permit and, later, for residence under the Employee of a Relocating Company category, if they do not meet any other criteria for residence.

Partners of New Zealand residents or citizens can be granted open work visas to allow them to remain with their partner while accumulating time to the 12 months required before a residence application can be made.

Highly skilled visa

The 'Silver Fern' visa is designed to attract highly-skilled long term immigrants aged 20 to 35. It is issued initially for nine months, extendable to two years after skilled work has been obtained. Applicants may then apply for residence. This option is limited to 300 applicants a year.

The long-term business visa

Those wishing to establish their own business or to buy a minimum 25% stake in an existing business can apply for a long term business visa or permit. As well as satisfying English language, health and character requirements, applicants must have:
1. Sufficient funds to support their business, themselves and their family.
2. A sound business plan (with realistic financial forecasts) which shows how the grant of the visa will be of benefit to New Zealand by:
    • Creating new employment opportunities.

- Saving a failed or failing company.
- Improving exports, or
- Introducing new, or expanding on existing business concepts, technologies, services or products.
- Relevant business experience or other expertise, including occupational registration where necessary, and
- A good record; no business failures in the previous five years and no involvement ever in business fraud or wrongdoing.

The long term business permit is issued initially for nine months but will be extended to three years provided the holder has started the business within the initial visa period.

Two years after establishing the business, the applicant may begin an application for residence under the Entrepreneur category, providing the business is successful.

The temporary retirement category

This is a two-year multiple entry visitor's visa available to applicants who are aged 66 and over, invest NZ$0.75 million in New Zealand for two years into an acceptable investment, demonstrate ownership of NZ$0.5 million of maintenance funds and an annual income of NZ$60,000 at the time of application, meet standard health and character requirements and hold and maintain comprehensive travel and/or health insurance for the duration of their stay.

They may include their partner in their application but not any dependent children.

New Zealand residence

The main paths to New Zealand residence are through the following categories:
1. Skilled migrant.
2. Investor.
3. Entrepreneur.
4. Family.

Skilled migrant category

The skilled migrant category operates on a points system with points awarded for qualifications, work experience, age, whether the person has a job offer and other settlement factors. In addition, applicants must satisfy health, character and English language proficiency standards. The process commences with an Expression of Interest. Only those who meet the appropriate criteria are invited to apply for residence.

Investor category:

The options are:
Investor One category: requires an investment of NZ$10 million for three years. No age restriction or English language requirement. Must stay in the country for at least 73 days in each of the last two years of the three-year period, and

Investor Two category: requires an investment of NZ$1.5 million for four years with settlement funds of $1 million (transfer not required). The applicant must be under 65, have at least three years' business experience and have some English language skills. Must stay in the country at least 146 days in each of the last three years of the four-year period.

Entrepreneur category

Persons who have a successful business that has been in operation for two years and who have decided that they wish to live in New Zealand permanently can apply directly for a residence permit under the Entrepreneur category.

Persons who are investing at least $500,000 and creating at least three new jobs can apply for residence under the Entrepreneur Plus category, earlier than the two years.

Family category

Applicants may be able to apply for residence depending on their family connections in New Zealand. The three options are:
1. **Partner category:** Living for 12 months with a New Zealand resident or citizen creates an opportunity to apply for residence on partnership grounds.
2. **Parent category:** The parents of a New Zealand citizen or resident may be eligible to apply for residence if they have a child or children who are eligible sponsors and either the sponsor or the parent has sufficient income and assets.
3. **Parent retirement category:** This is available to those with family links to New Zealand who are able to make a significant contribution to the New Zealand economy. To qualify the applicant must have an adult child who lives in New Zealand and is either a New Zealand citizen or resident for at least three years; invest NZ$1 million for four years into an acceptable investment, demonstrate ownership of NZ$0.5 million of settlement funds and an annual income of NZ$60,000 at the time of application and meet standard health and character requirements.

Once residence is granted

With the first resident visa come travel rights which are valid for two years. This allows the resident to leave New Zealand temporarily without endangering his or her residence status.

At the end of the two years, residents can apply for a Permanent Resident Visa allowing multiple trips into and out of New Zealand for at least the life of their passport and currently transferable to their next passport. Eligibility depends on:
1. The amount of time spent in New Zealand during the first two years, or
2. Holding New Zealand tax resident status, or
3. Having established a business which has been trading for at least a year, or
4. Having an acceptable level of investment in New Zealand, or
5. Having a family base in New Zealand.

Citizenship

To qualify for citizenship, the applicant must have been resident for at least five years, be free of any convictions and have:
1. Been present in New Zealand for at least 1,350 days during the five years immediately preceding the application.
2. Been present in New Zealand for at least 240 days in each of these five years.

Immigration advice

The only people legally able to give immigration advice in New Zealand are solicitors and licensed immigration advisers. While there are a few exceptions, it is important that you establish the credentials of your adviser as Immigration will not accept applications where the advice has come from someone either unlicensed or not specifically exempted from holding a licence. This requirement applies to advice given from off-shore.

Chapter 9: Overseas Business Risk in New Zealand

New Zealand poses very little risk to the visiting business person in the political and economic arenas.

New Zealand is a parliamentary democracy and a constitutional monarchy with Queen Elizabeth II as the Queen of New Zealand. Elections are held every three years under a Mixed Member Proportional (MMP) system. The New Zealand National Party is the largest partner in the National-led Government and is lead by current Party Leader and Prime Minister of New Zealand John Key. The Opposition is the New Zealand Labour Party led by David Shearer.

New Zealand has a mixed economy which operates on free market principles. It has sizeable manufacturing and service sectors complementing a highly efficient agricultural sector. Exports of goods and services account for around one third of real expenditure GDP.

Human Rights

The Human Rights Commission of New Zealand conducted a full report in 2010 "Human Rights in New Zealand" and found that New Zealand continues to meet human rights standards. It also identified thirty priority areas where further action is essential to strengthen human rights protections.

There are two main pieces of law in New Zealand that specifically promote and protect human rights. One is the Human Rights Act 1993, and the other is the New Zealand Bill of Rights Act 1990.

In respect of human rights and the Treaty of Waitangi in New Zealand today, there are legislative mechanisms in place to protect the principles of the Treaty and the rights of Māori as Indigenous people. In practice, the level of recognition and protection varies. There has been significant progress in hearing and settling Treaty claims, revitalising the reo Māori and establishing whānau-centred initiatives, particularly in health and education.

Terrorism Threat

There is a low threat of terrorism in New Zealand. However, there is a global risk of terrorism from which New Zealand is not exempt.

The Centre for the Protection of National Infrastructure also provides protective security advice to businesses.

Organised Crime

There are some instances of street crime in urban areas. Thefts can occur in major tourist areas especially from camper vans, unattended vehicles or tourist accommodation. It is advised never to leave items of value in unattended vehicles.

Chapter 10: Starting a Business in New Zealand

Four main avenues are open to overseas entities wishing to set up a business in New Zealand. They are to:
1. Register a branch.
2. Form a subsidiary company.
3. Merge with or take over an existing New Zealand company, or
4. Enter a limited partnership.

Registering a branch

An overseas company wishing to register a branch in New Zealand must reserve its name with the Registrar of Companies and file a registration application within 10 working days from the start of business. The application must include:
1. The names and current residential addresses of the directors of the overseas company.
2. The address of the overseas company's main place of business in New Zealand.
3. Evidence of the overseas company's incorporation and a copy of the instrument constituting or defining its constitution (in English), and
4. The name and address of at least one person in New Zealand who is authorised to accept service of documents on the company's behalf.

Australian companies wishing to register a branch in New Zealand benefit from an information sharing arrangement between the Companies Office and ASIC. Registration is cheaper (if done online) than for companies from other countries, and you are only required to provide in your application, the company's Australian Company Number (ACN), together with the following New Zealand-specific details:

1. An active email address.
2. The name reserved for the company with the Companies Office (this must be identical to the company's name as it is registered with ASIC)
3. Physical addresses of the company's principal place of business in New Zealand and person(s) authorised to accept service in New Zealand, and
4. An address (postal or physical) for communications (with the Registrar).

Australian overseas companies also benefit on an ongoing basis from reduced compliance requirements. For example, they need only file a simplified annual return, with ASIC supplying the Companies Office on request with the relevant information filed by the company in Australia.

Forming and registering a subsidiary company

A subsidiary company incorporated in New Zealand must have non-resident shareholders and directors, although a pending law change will require at least one director to be resident in New Zealand or Australia. Generally, any legal entity may be a shareholder, but only individuals may be appointed directors. There is no statutory requirement to appoint a company secretary.

There is no restriction on the size of a company's share capital. Companies (other than cooperatives) are not permitted to have a par or nominal value attached to their shares. Instead, company directors are required to determine the consideration for the issue of shares, and to resolve (and, if they vote in favour of the issue, certify) that the consideration and terms of issue are fair and reasonable (in their opinion) to the company and all existing shareholders. It is not necessary for the issue price to be fully paid, although shareholders are liable to creditors (and liquidators) to the extent of any amounts unpaid on their shares.

As with a branch, the first step to register a subsidiary is to apply to reserve the proposed subsidiary's name. Once the name has been approved and reserved with the Registrar, the following incorporation documents must be filed:
1. Consent to act as a director and (for each director) a certificate that he or she is not disqualified from acting.
2. Consent of the shareholder (for each shareholder).
3. The notice reserving the company's name.
4. A copy of the constitution, if the company is to have one.

Applications to the Registrar must also include:
1. The name and residential address of each director.
2. Similar details for the proposed shareholders and the number of shares to be issued respectively to them.
3. Details of the registered office and address for service of documents, both of which must be in New Zealand.

A branch or a subsidiary

The decision whether to establish a branch office or a subsidiary company will be influenced by legal, tax and commercial considerations. The following issues may be relevant:

1. Annual accounts

A New Zealand branch of an overseas company must file two separate sets of audited financial statements, one for its worldwide operations and one for its New Zealand business. A subsidiary is required to file audited financial statements relating to its New Zealand business only. Every company must file an annual return at the Companies Office.

2. Filing of documents

Any changes to incorporation or branch documents must be notified to the Registrar within stipulated time frames, which can be as short as 10 working days. This requirement may prove more cumbersome for a branch than for a subsidiary as subsidiaries can file all documents except financial statements online whereas branches must file physical copies of all documents.

3. Liability

A New Zealand branch (being legally the overseas company), bears directly any liabilities that it may incur under New Zealand law. There is no sheltering of liability behind a different legal persona. Establishing a special purpose company as the branch may help ring-fence this liability. In practice, however, limited liability may be illusory as, unless the subsidiary is of substance in its own right, any significant commercial dealings may need to be guaranteed by the overseas parent.

4. Tax

A New Zealand branch of an overseas company will generally be considered non-resident for taxation purposes. If an overseas company incorporates a subsidiary in New Zealand, that subsidiary is a New Zealand tax resident.

5. Fees

Filing fees to reserve a company name are NZ$10.22, and to register an overseas company, NZ$150.00.

Merger or takeover proposal

A company considering merging with or buying a New Zealand company must be aware of the restrictions on business acquisitions contained in the Commerce Act 1986.

If the New Zealand company is listed on the New Zealand stock exchange or, if not listed, has more than 50 shareholders, and share parcels, the Takeovers Code is likely to apply. Specific advice on the implications of the Code should be sought.

Forming a limited partnership

From an investor's perspective, a limited partnership provides the limited liability protection of a company and some of the flow through tax and confidentiality advantages of a partnership. The New Zealand limited partnership model is broadly comparable to limited partnerships in other jurisdictions, including Delaware, Australian states and the Channel Islands. The following issues may be relevant in deciding whether to establish a limited partnership:

1. Confidentiality

Although the identity of the limited partners must be registered with the Registrar, that information is not publicly disclosed. Every limited partnership must have a limited partnership agreement.

Unlike a company's constitution, however, this agreement is not registered with the Registrar and is not made public.

2. Liability

Like a company, a limited partnership is a separate legal entity from its investors; which separation helps to protect those investors from losses and claims arising from the business activities of the limited partnership. Limited partners are passive investors and their liability is typically limited to the capital they agree to contribute, provided they do not take part in the management of the limited partnership. The general partner manages the business and is responsible for the debts and obligations of the limited partnership if the limited partnership itself cannot meet them. A general partner may be a company.

3. Tax

Limited partnerships are treated as fiscally transparent for New Zealand tax purposes, notwithstanding their separate legal identity. The limited partners are treated as holding the assets of the limited partnership, and personally derive the income and deductions. This presents a number of tax advantages, such as the ability to distribute capital gains tax free to the limited partners and the pass through of tax losses (although the losses claimable by a limited partner are effectively capped at the amount of that limited partner's economic exposure to those losses). Use of a limited partnership can involve additional tax issues in some circumstances, such as where partnership interests are traded or where non-residents are involved, although these can usually be resolved.

4. Flexibility

There is no restriction on the potential business activities of a limited partnership. Although a limited partnership is a creation of statute, in comparison with a company, the limited partnership is much less regulated.

5. Accounts

While a limited partnership is required to prepare accounts (and keep them at its registered office), generally they are not required to file those accounts with the Registrar and therefore the accounts are not made public.

6. Fees

The filing fees for establishing a limited partnership electronically are NZ$270.00 as at October 2012.

7. Filing of documents

The Registrar must be notified within 10 days of any changes to the details lodged on initial registration.

Chapter 11: Overseas Investment Regime

New Zealand welcomes foreign investment although the consent of the Overseas Investment Office (OIO) is required for certain transactions involving "overseas persons". The screening regime is contained within the Overseas Investment Act 2005 (Act).

An overseas person is defined as:

- An individual who is not a New Zealand citizen and who is not ordinarily resident in New Zealand.
- Partnership, body corporate or trust where an overseas person or persons have 25% or more ownership or control

The Act applies to acquisitions by overseas persons of 25% or more direct or indirect ownership and/or control of interests in:
1. Significant business assets.
2. "Sensitive" and "special" New Zealand land
   - Farm land, and
   - Fishing quota.

Business assets

An overseas person can require consent for business acquisitions (not involving sensitive land) where:
1. If establishing a new business, the total expenditure involved exceeds NZ$100m.
2. If buying an existing business through an assets deal, the price paid (either by one transaction or a series of related transactions) exceeds NZ$100m, or.

3. If buying an existing business through a share deal, either the amount paid for the shares, or the gross value of the New Zealand assets of the target company (including its 25% or more subsidiaries), exceeds NZ$100m.

For Australian non-government investors, the current threshold is NZ$477m. This amount is adjusted each year to reflect movements in GDP in each country.

There are a number of exemptions to the requirement to obtain consent that are contained in the Overseas Investment Regulations 2005 (Regulations). These can be viewed on the OIO's website.

Overseas investment in sensitive land

Overseas persons wishing to buy sensitive land will require Ministerial approval. This applies to both freehold interests in the land and to a lease for a term of three years or more (including rights of renewal). To secure consent, the overseas investor will need to demonstrate that the purchase will bring benefits which are incremental to those which would result from continued New Zealand ownership.

Briefly, land will be sensitive if it is, or includes:
1. Non-urban land over five hectares in area.
2. The foreshore or seabed.
3. Land on certain named islands if the land is over 0.4 hectares
4. land on any other islands excluding the North or South Island (regardless of the land area involved)
5. Any land which is over 0.4 hectares and:
   - Is the bed of a lake.
   - Is held for conservation purposes under the Conservation Act 1987.

- Is earmarked in a district or proposed district plan to be used as a reserve, a public park, for recreation purposes or as open space.
- Is subject to a heritage order or a requirement under the Resource Management Act 1991 or the Historic Places Act 1993.
- Is an historic place or area or wāhi tapu (site sacred to Māori) which is registered or the subject of an application to register under the Historic Places Act 1993, and
- Any land which is over 0.2 hectares and adjoins the foreshore.

Land will also be sensitive if it is over 0.4 hectares and adjoins:
1. The bed of a lake.
2. Land held for conservation purposes under the Conservation Act 1987 if the conservation land is itself over 0.4 hectares.
3. Any scientific, scenic, historic or nature reserve under the Reserves Act 1977 that is itself over 0.4 hectares.
4. Any regional park.
5. Any land listed as a reserve or a park by the OIO.
6. Land over 0.4 hectares that adjoins the sea or a lake and is an esplanade reserve, a recreation reserve, a road or a Māori reservation.
7. Land over 0.4 hectares that is subject to a heritage order or requirement for a heritage order, and
8. Land over 0.4 hectares that includes a historic place, historic area (which is itself over 0.4 hectares) or wāhi tapu.

The definition of sensitive land is very detailed and, as such, requires careful checking and analysis from qualified advisers. In particular, it may be "sensitive" by association if it adjoins any of the types of land listed previously, or is "associated" with other land already controlled by an overseas person. Advice should also be sought on how to meet the incremental benefit test.

Special land

Special land is defined in the Regulations as the foreshore, seabed, riverbed or lakebed. If an investor wishes to acquire sensitive land under the Act and that sensitive land includes any special land, the special land must first be offered to the Government by the owner. The Government can acquire only that part of the sensitive land that is special land and can acquire it only if the overseas person actually completes the acquisition of the sensitive land.

The general policy approach is to acquire the land only if there is a public interest in the Government owning it. Criteria include: whether there is a "recognised attitude" among New Zealanders or a group of New Zealanders toward the land; the inter-relationship of the land with the surrounding area; whether there is a more cost-effective alternative to government ownership; whether the benefits exceed the costs; and whether government purchase will adversely affect the overseas person's ability to carry out the investment.

Overseas investment in farm land

Where a proposed acquisition involves farm land (being land that is used exclusively or principally for agricultural, horticultural or pastoral purposes, or for the keeping of bees, poultry or livestock), that farm land must first have been offered by the vendor on the open market to persons who are not overseas persons in accordance with the procedures set out in the Regulations.

60

Exemptions from this requirement can be obtained, but only in special circumstances and at the discretion of the relevant Minister.

The consent process

All applications for consent must be tested against the prescribed investment criteria set out in the Act and Regulations. An applicant (or if the applicant is not an individual, the persons with control of the applicant) must:
1. Be of good character.
2. Have relevant business experience or acumen, and
3. Be able to demonstrate a financial commitment to the investment.

Additional criteria for sensitive land

Applications for overseas investment in sensitive land must also satisfy the following additional criteria.

Either:

1. The applicant, or if the applicant is not an individual, all the individuals who control the applicant, are New Zealand citizens, ordinarily resident in New Zealand, or are intending to reside in New Zealand indefinitely and have applied for a visa or permit under any of Immigration New Zealand's residence policies.
2. The overseas investment will, or is likely to, benefit New Zealand (or any part of it or group of New Zealanders), as determined by the relevant Ministers.
3. If the relevant land includes non-urban land that in area (either alone or together with any associated land) exceeds five

hectares, the relevant Ministers determine that the benefit will be, or is likely to be, substantial and identifiable.

4. The applicant submits a detailed business plan that addresses the "benefits to New Zealand" factors set out in the Regulations. Such benefits can be longer term as well as immediate.

Processing and decision application

The OIO is responsible for overseeing the Act, and assesses consent applications. The OIO will commonly contact the applicant or its advisers for further information during the process. The power to make decisions on whether to approve or decline an application is vested in the relevant Minister of the Crown. The Ministers have delegated to the OIO the power to decide all applications except those involving sensitive rural land and land adjoining waterways.

There is no mandatory timeframe within which the OIO/Ministers must make a decision. Consent applications can take several months; typically two to three months for a business acquisition and three to four months for a sensitive land acquisition, longer if the application is complex. Potential consent requirements should be assessed early when considering a foreign investment in New Zealand.

Consent conditions

Consent is usually granted subject to various conditions with which the applicant must comply. When imposing conditions of consent, the OIO must be satisfied that the condition is necessary and will achieve the desired result. Conditions can be varied or revoked in appropriate circumstances.

Compliance will be monitored by the OIO and will continue until the benefits of the investment have been realised or the conditions have been revoked. The Government has instructed the OIO that in general, monitoring should not extend beyond five years unless the benefits are not expected to begin accruing until after that time.

Penalties apply in case of a breach of these provisions. In addition, the High Court has the power, on application from the OIO, to order disposal of any property (which includes a right or interest in any security, an interest in land, an interest in fishing quota or any other property or any rights or interests in any other property).

Chapter 12: Taxation in New Zealand

New Zealand has a broad-based tax system consisting principally of:
1. Income tax
2. Fringe benefit tax
3. Resident and non-resident withholding tax (RWT and NRWT)
4. Goods and services tax (GST)
5. Accident Compensation levies
6. Import tariffs and miscellaneous excise duties, and
7. Local authority rates on property.

Stamp duty, gift duty and death duties are not payable in New Zealand.

Tax advice provided by lawyers enjoys legal privilege, meaning that it does not have to be disclosed to the authorities in most circumstances.

For individuals and companies defined as "resident" in New Zealand, income tax is imposed on worldwide income. Non-resident individuals and companies, on the other hand, are taxed only on income derived from New Zealand, and their tax liability may be reduced by the provisions of an applicable double tax agreement.

Individuals are regarded as resident in New Zealand for income tax purposes if they have a permanent place of abode in New Zealand or are present in New Zealand for more than 183 days within a 12-month period.

A company is regarded as resident in New Zealand if it:
1. Is incorporated in New Zealand.
2. Has its head office in New Zealand.
3. Has its centre of management in New Zealand.
4. Is controlled by its directors in New Zealand.

Companies (both resident and non-resident) are taxed at 28%. Individuals (both resident and non-resident) are taxed incrementally at between 10.5% and 33%. As noted above, non-residents are taxed only on their New Zealand-sourced income.

For individuals, assessable income includes (among other items) salary and wages, bonuses, other employment benefits or remuneration, partnership income and investment income. For salary and wage earners, tax is deducted at source through the Pay As You Earn (PAYE) system. Non-cash benefits provided to employees are subject to fringe benefit tax which is payable by the employer.

For companies, net income generally corresponds with accounting profit or loss. However, adjustments are commonly required in relation to:
1. The timing of income and expenditure recognition.
2. Bad debts, and
3. Various provisions and reserves.

New Zealand does not generally tax capital gains. In certain circumstances, however, the proceeds from the sale of real or personal property (including shares) may be subject to income tax (for example, where the dominant purpose of the initial purchase was to resell the property at a profit).

Double tax agreements

New Zealand has entered into double tax agreements (or tax treaties) with more than 30 countries to reduce the incidence of double taxation and to provide more certainty for taxpayers operating in foreign jurisdictions. Foreign tax credits are generally available to New Zealand residents for foreign income tax imposed on income derived from countries or territories outside New Zealand. The availability and quantum of the foreign tax credit is subject to certain limitations, but does not depend on New Zealand having entered into a double tax agreement with the particular country or territory concerned.

Treatment of tax losses

If a resident company or a New Zealand branch of a non-resident company incurs a tax loss, that loss can generally be carried forward (indefinitely) to offset future New Zealand net income and shared between group companies, provided a certain level of shareholder continuity (or in the case of group companies, common ownership) is maintained. Individuals and trusts can also carry forward tax losses, but these losses are effectively "trapped" and cannot be shared with other entities.

Taxation of dividends paid by resident companies to residents

Dividends paid by resident companies to residents are, in most instances, taxable to the shareholder. However, dividends paid between New Zealand resident companies that are part of the same wholly-owned group are generally exempt (subject to certain other requirements).

To avoid the double payment of tax on the same income (i.e. by the company and the shareholder when the company's income is distributed as a dividend) imputation credits may be attached to dividends paid by resident companies (to both residents and non-residents). An imputation credit represents a portion of the tax paid by the company (for every $1 of tax paid, a company receives a $1 imputation credit which it can attach to dividends). Imputation credits received by resident shareholders (companies and individuals) are offset against any tax payable on their income, including tax on dividends received.

Subject to certain exceptions, a dividend paid by a resident company to a resident is subject to a 33% withholding tax, although the withholding tax liability is reduced by any imputation credits attached to the dividend. If the dividend is fully imputed (i.e. imputation credits are attached at the maximum rate) only a residual 3% withholding tax will be imposed on the dividend.

Portfolio Investments Entities (PIE)

Widely held investment entities which are tax resident in New Zealand can take advantage of New Zealand's PIE tax regime. Broadly speaking, to qualify as a PIE, they must be widely held (or owned by widely held vehicles) and cannot hold more than 20% of any company or unit trust they invest into (subject to some exceptions).

A PIE is exempt from tax on gains from the sale of shares in New Zealand resident companies, and in Australian companies that are listed on an approved Australian Securities Exchange index.

PIES are not taxed like companies. Instead their income is taxed only once either to the PIE (if the investor is an individual) or to

68

the investor (if the investor is a company or another PIE). For individuals, the PIE pays tax at a rate no higher than 28%.

Non-resident investors in PIEs pay no tax on income from outside New Zealand.

Taxation of investments by New Zealand residents in non-resident entities

Generally, income from 10% or greater stakes in New Zealand-controlled foreign companies (CFCs) is not subject to New Zealand tax as earned unless it is passive income. When distributed to a New Zealand shareholder, it is taxable unless the shareholder is a company. Income from foreign investment funds (FIFs) is generally calculated either using a "fair dividend rate" or a comparative value method. The fair dividend rate method taxes the shareholder on deemed income of 5% of the value of the investment. The comparative value method taxes appreciation during the year plus distributions. There are significant exemptions from both regimes for investment in Australian companies.

Taxation of payments to non-residents

Payments of dividends, interest and royalties to individuals or companies not resident in New Zealand are generally subject to non-resident withholding tax (NRWT). The rate of NRWT imposed depends upon the type of payment and whether a double tax agreement (DTA) is in place:

Double tax agreement countries		Other countries
Dividends*	0-15%	0-30%*
Interest	10-15%	15%**
Royalties	5-15%	15%

A 0% rate of NRWT applies to fully imputed dividends paid to a non-resident shareholder holding a 10% or more direct voting interest in a New Zealand company or holding less than 10% but whose post-treaty rate is less than 15%. To the extent the dividend is not fully imputed, NRWT will be required to be withheld at 30% (reduced to 15% for countries New Zealand has a DTA with).

Where interest is paid to a non-resident and a resident (jointly) the applicable rate of NRWT will be higher than 15%.

In the case of dividends, certain royalty payments, and interest paid to non-associated persons, NRWT is generally a final tax for New Zealand tax purposes.

The Foreign Investor Tax Credit (FITC) regime alters the NRWT regime by effectively eliminating the monetary effect of NRWT on dividends paid by a New Zealand company to a non-resident shareholder who holds a direct voting interest in a New Zealand company of less than 10% and the post-treaty tax rate for the initial dividend is 15% or more.

The FITC regime achieves this by providing a tax credit to the New Zealand resident company, which the resident company must use to fund an additional "supplementary dividend" to the non-resident (which is equal to the NRWT payable where the dividend is fully imputed). This ensures that the non-resident shareholder is in a no less beneficial position than a New Zealand resident shareholder receiving the same dividend.

In respect of interest payments made by an approved New Zealand borrower (Approved Issuer) to a non-associated non-resident lender, the NRWT rate can be reduced to 0%, provided certain conditions and registration formalities are satisfied.

Approved Issuers must generally pay a levy (Approved Issuer Levy or AIL) equivalent to 2% of the interest for the right to pay zero-rated interest.

Interest paid on certain qualifying widely held bonds may be eligible for a 0% rate of NRWT without the payer of the interest having to pay AIL.

Withholding tax is deducted at the rate of 15% from non-resident contractors for certain work or services performed in New Zealand (this rate increases to 20% where the non-resident contractor does not provide a prescribed withholding declaration to the payer prior to the payment being made). An exemption certificate removing the need for the withholding deduction can be granted by the IRD in certain circumstances.

Transfer pricing and thin capitalisation

New Zealand's transfer pricing regime seeks to protect the New Zealand tax base by ensuring that cross-border transactions are priced (at least for tax purposes) on an arm's length basis. New Zealand also has thin capitalisation rules which, broadly speaking, disallow certain interest deductions for a foreign owned New Zealand group (depending on their debt to equity ratio) or for New Zealand residents with an income interest in a CFC or who control a resident company with such an interest.

Goods and Services Tax (GST)

GST is a consumption tax charged at 15% on the supply of most goods and services in New Zealand. GST-registered taxpayers must charge GST on the goods and services they supply and can obtain a credit for any GST they pay in the course of their business. In this way, the burden of GST is passed along a chain of registered suppliers until it reaches the final consumer.

Those making supplies in New Zealand are required to register for GST if they carry on a taxable activity (which is similar in concept to a business, but wider in scope) through which they will make taxable supplies of more than NZ$60,000 per year. A person carrying on a taxable activity (whether in New Zealand or outside New Zealand) can voluntarily register for GST even if they are under this threshold.

Certain supplies of goods and services can be either exempt from GST or zero-rated (e.g. the supply of financial services, services performed as an employee, some services supplied to non-residents and supplies wholly or partly consisting of land.

Accident Compensation Levies

New Zealand operates a no-fault accident compensation scheme whereby persons suffering from accidental injuries need not prove fault before receiving compensation. The scheme provides for some financial assistance for medical expenses, loss of earnings, and compensation for dependants in the case of death. All compensation is paid by the Accident Compensation Corporation (ACC), which is funded by:

1. Levies paid by all employers, self-employed persons and private domestic workers for work-related accidents. The levy for the self-employed and private domestic workers is set by regulation, whereas the levy for employers is determined by the industry risk class applying to the employer, and may be adjusted up or down depending on the individual employer's safety management practices.

2. Levies paid by self-employed persons, private domestic workers and employees for non-work related accidents.
3. A residual claims levy paid by employers, private domestic workers and the self-employed to cover claims outstanding prior to the introduction of the Accident Compensation Act 2001, and
4. Funds set aside by Parliament to fund compensation for injuries to non-earners.

Another option is the ACC's accredited employer programme under which employers can elect to pay a reduced levy, in return for funding all or a share of any compensation entitlements incurred at their workplace. To be accepted for the programme, the employer must satisfy a number of criteria, including a minimum level of safety expertise and financial solvency.

Import duties

Import licensing, once a common means of sheltering New Zealand producers, no longer exists in New Zealand, with tariffs now the principal form of protection.

Over recent years, there has been a steady reduction of tariff rates for goods imported into New Zealand. Tariff rates vary from item to item and depend upon the country of origin, with preferential rates being applied to Australia, Canada, "least-developed countries", "less-developed countries" and Pacific Forum countries. Items that are outside the scope of local manufacturing are generally duty free, or may qualify for a duty concession.

Where New Zealand is party to a free trade agreement (FTA), the FTA will address in detail the tariffs applicable between the two countries.

Goods and Services Tax (GST) know in the UK and US as VAT is also charged on any goods which are imported into New Zealand. An input tax credit can be claimed for this GST (meaning no net cost arises) where the importer is GST-registered and is acquiring the imported goods for the purpose of making supplies which are subject to GST.

Rates

Rates are the main source of local government revenue. These are calculated as a percentage of the value of land and/or capital improvements.

Chapter 13: Regulations Affecting Business in New Zealand

The following is intended to give you a general flavour of New Zealand's business regulation. It is not an exhaustive list and does not cover industry-specific legislation. You should seek specific advice about whether and how the legal framework will affect your plans.

Competition law

The Commerce Act 1986:
- Regulates business acquisitions
- Prohibits restrictive trade practices, and
- Allows price controls to be imposed in certain industries.

Business acquisitions

Part 3 of the Commerce Act prohibits the purchase of shares in or assets of a business where the acquisition would have (or would be likely to have) the effect of substantially lessening competition in a market.

The threshold is triggered by an increase in the scope for the exercise of unilateral or coordinated market power, evidenced by a change in market circumstances that renders coordination between remaining firms more likely.

Specifically, the New Zealand Commerce Commission; the authority which administers the Commerce Act looks for increases in the scope to raise price and/or reduce product quality or service, relative to what would have occurred in the absence of the acquisition. Relevant to this are the market share of the merged entity, the market shares of other participants, the likelihood of new entry, the merged entity's relationship with suppliers and purchasers, and whether there are features of the market which are suggestive of the potential for collusion and discipline.

The Commerce Commission has issued two "safe harbours" for assessing horizontal aggregation. An acquisition is unlikely to raise Commerce Act concerns if, after the acquisition:
1. The three largest firms in the market have a combined market share of less than 70% and the merged entity has a market share of less than 40%, or
2. The three largest firms in the market have a combined market share of more than 70% and the merged entity has a market share of less than 20%.

The safe harbours are only a starting point for the analysis. Falling outside the safe harbours does not mean an acquisition necessarily lessens competition. For example, market shares may be high but there may be few barriers to entry or expansion. Those taking comfort from the safe-harbours should adopt the market definitions likely to be adopted by the Commerce Commission.

Maximum penalties for an acquisition in breach of the Commerce Act are:
1. NZ$500,000 for individuals, and
2. NZ$5 million for companies, as well as an order requiring divestment of specified assets or shares.

Restrictive trade practices

Part 2 of the Commerce Act is designed to regulate restrictive trade practices arising either collusively (between two or more parties) or unilaterally on the part of a firm which holds a substantial degree of market power.

The following practices are prohibited (unless explicitly authorised by the Commerce Commission on public benefit grounds):
1. Any contracts, arrangements or understandings which have the purpose, effect, or likely effect of substantially lessening competition in a market.
2. Price-fixing and market-sharing arrangements.
3. Collective boycotts between competitors which prevent or restrict trade, resulting in a substantial lessening of competition.
4. Resale price maintenance arrangements by which suppliers of goods set and enforce sale prices to be charged by re-sellers, and
5. Taking advantage of a substantial degree of market power in a market (which can include trans-Tasman markets) for the purpose of restricting entry into a market, deterring competitive conduct, or eliminating a competitor from a market.

Engaging in a prohibited practice may result in a penalty of:
1. Up to NZ$500,000 for individuals, and
2. The greater of NZ$10 million or either three times the value of any commercial gain resulting from the contravention (if it can be easily ascertained) or 10% of the turnover of the body corporate and all its related bodies corporate.

Price controls

Part 4 of the Commerce Act contains a mechanism to impose price controls on particular goods and services. There are no restrictions on the industries to which Part 4 may apply.

Part 4A requires the Commerce Commission to establish performance thresholds for electricity line businesses and gives the Commission the ability to impose price controls on businesses which breach those thresholds.

Other industries subject to specific market regulation include:
1. Telecommunications (under the Telecommunications Act 2001)
2. Dairy (under the Dairy Industry Restructuring Act 2001)
3. Gas (under the Commerce Act 1992).

Consumer protection

Provision of goods and services to consumers

The principal pieces of consumer protection legislation are the Fair Trading Act 1986 and the Consumer Guarantees Act 1993.

The Fair Trading Act

The Fair Trading Act applies to anyone involved "in trade". It prohibits (generally whether the activity is intentional or not):
1. Engaging in conduct which is likely to mislead or deceive.
2. Engaging in conduct that is liable to mislead as to the nature, manufacturing process, characteristics, suitability for purpose, or quantity of goods.

3. Engaging in conduct that is liable to mislead as to the nature, characteristics, suitability for purpose, or quantity of services.
4. Engaging in misleading conduct in relation to employment that is or may be offered to a person, and
5. Making false or misleading representations in respect of goods or services.

The Fair Trading Act also deals with consumer information, falsely applying trademarks, using coercion in connection with supply, offering prizes without providing them as offered, bait advertising, pyramid selling schemes, consumer information standards, product and service safety standards, product recall and the sale of unsafe goods. The Act is enforced by the Commerce Commission and gives consumers direct rights of action. Anyone providing goods or services needs to be aware of the Act.

The Consumer Guarantees Act:

1. Provides consumers with certain basic warranties in relation to goods and services.
2. Sets out certain guarantees that relate to the quality, suitability and other aspects of goods and services, and
3. Gives consumers remedies against suppliers where goods or services fail to comply with one or more of those guarantees.

The Act does not apply to dealings with business customers and commercial contracts usually contain a specific acknowledgment of this effect. It applies only to persons buying goods or services for the purposes of household or domestic use.

Remedies include damages and the right to cancel a contract.

Generally, New Zealand's consumer protection regime is similar to that of many comparable jurisdictions, but there are some points of difference:

1. There are no cease and desist provisions to stop a trader engaging in potentially harmful conduct, and
2. There is no power to stop recidivist offenders from trading.

Consumer credit

Providing credit at the consumer level through credit contracts and hire purchase agreements is regulated by the Credit Contracts and Consumer Finance Act 2003. The Act sets out disclosure requirements for contracts and allows debtors to have the terms of a contract changed for reasons of hardship. It also allows the courts to re-open and vary "oppressive" contracts.

Retail regulation

Many other laws and regulations affect the operation of retail businesses, including:

1. Smoke free legislation.
2. Restrictions on the sale of liquor.
3. Restrictions on shop trading days (but only three and a half days of the year have restrictions)
4. Weights and measures standards, and
5. Food safety and labelling legislation.

Contract law

New Zealand contract law is light handed, and allows contracting parties' significant freedom in concluding their bargain.

In terms of form, all contracts can be concluded orally, other than those involving land, mortgages, consumer guarantees or employment agreements, which must be written. There is substantial freedom in terms of content. That said certain contracts may be supplemented by terms implied by various statutes. The Sale of Goods Act 1908, for example, sets out various terms that are read into contracts for the sale of commercial goods unless the parties clearly intended otherwise.

Other context-specific pieces of legislation:

1. The Minors' Contracts Act 1969, which protects minors (unmarried persons under the age of 18) from commercial exploitation. A contract with a minor cannot be enforced unless it is fair and reasonable, and
2. The Contractual Remedies Act 1979, which allows a party to cancel a contract for a misrepresentation (if prescribed criteria are satisfied), and recover damages. The courts also have the power to grant other types of relief under the Act.

Several common law rights of recourse also exist for misleading conduct and/or statements.

Public protection

New Zealand has legislated, like many other countries, to protect various rights of the public at large.

Information privacy

The Privacy Act 1993 aims to protect the confidentiality of personal information by limiting the purposes for which it can be used and disseminated and by giving individuals a right of access to personal information held about them.

Human rights

The Human Rights Act 1993 generally accords with United Nations covenants and conventions on human rights. The Act:
1. Makes it unlawful to discriminate in relation to employment or the provision of goods or services on the grounds of sex, marital status, religious or ethical belief, colour, race, ethnic or national origins, disability, age, political opinion, employment status, family status or sexual orientation.
2. Prohibits sexual and racial harassment and the incitement of racial disharmony, and
3. Prohibits publishing or displaying any advertisement or notice which indicates an intention to commit a breach of any of the provisions of the Act.

Gambling

The Gambling Act 2003 prohibits gambling unless it is authorised under the Act.

"Gambling" involves (broadly) staking money (or money's worth) directly or indirectly on an outcome that depends at least partly on chance, where a prize is involved. You should seek specialist advice if you plan on setting up a gambling business (whether as a primary or ancillary part of your proposed business).

Creditor protection

The Personal Property Securities Act 1999 allows creditors to give notice of a security interest they hold over property held by debtors by registering a "financing statement" on a public (online) register. A range of security interests are registered, including in relation to fixed and floating charges, chattel mortgages, hire purchase agreements, finance leases and retention of title arrangements. Registration is vital in determining the validity and priority of a creditor's interest.

Chapter 14: Buying and Developing Property

New Zealand uses the Torrens land registration system under which most parcels of land have their own titles showing dimensions and location, and recording ownership and other interests affecting the land. The Government guarantees the accuracy of titles, which can be searched by the public for a nominal fee.

The primary attraction of the Torrens system is that dealings can be conducted in reliance on a single title, rather than on a succession of title deeds. New Zealand has converted almost all titles, plans and instruments into an electronic format, allowing real-time searching and electronic registration of all land title and surveying transactions.

Under New Zealand law, buildings and other improvements permanently attached to the land form part of the land itself and pass with ownership of the land, unless the current owner and a purchaser agree otherwise.

Contracts for sale and purchase of land

To be enforceable under New Zealand law, a contract for the sale and purchase of land must be in writing and signed by the parties involved or their authorised agents.

Once signed, an agreement for sale and purchase becomes legally binding on all parties. It can, however, be made subject to conditions which protect the seller or buyer.

Common conditions are:
1. The buyer raising finance.
2. The buyer being satisfied with valuation, local authority information relating to the land, engineering reports and building reports.
3. The buyer being satisfied with the title.

Where a real estate agent is engaged by a seller to effect a sale, commission is payable by the seller, typically at a rate of 4% of the purchase price up to NZ$250,000 and 2% thereafter (plus GST). There is no stamp duty.

Dealings with land are registered electronically against the title.

Resource Management Act and district plans

The Resource Management Act 1991 (RMA) is New Zealand's principal statute relating to the use of land, water, minerals, the coast, air and physical resources. The Act aims to promote "sustainable management of physical and natural resources". The Act also seeks to maintain and enhance New Zealand's "clean, green" image.

The RMA has major implications for industrial projects and property developments. A new development may require a number of consents under the Act before it can go ahead.

Controls on development are administered by locally elected government authorities and are expressed through a range of publicly notified plans. These include regional plans, regional coastal plans and district plans. Plans set out rules for activities in various locations or "zones". Parties seeking consent to proceed with a development must follow the procedures set out in the relevant plan, and this may involve public participation through the public notification of the consent application.

Privately owned land may be designated in the district plan as being required by the Government for a public work, which may result in the land being acquired by the Government (compulsorily if necessary). The current market value of the land would be paid as compensation.

Building works

The Building Act 2004 is designed to regulate and control building work and the use of buildings. Every new building and most substantial alterations or additions to existing buildings will require a building consent. Multiple-use approvals are available for group home builders who build homes throughout New Zealand using the same or similar plans.

On completion of works, a code compliance certificate will be issued, provided compliance with the building consent has been satisfied.

Allied to the Building Act is the Building Code. This sets criteria to ensure buildings are safe, sanitary, have adequate means of escape and, in the case of public buildings, have access and facilities for disabled persons. Existing buildings, which are being altered, may require upgrading in the course of the alterations in order to comply with these criteria as nearly as is reasonably practicable. Buildings considered earthquake prone may also be required to be upgraded.

The Act imposes restrictions upon occupation of a building where public areas of that building are subject to building works for which a code compliance certificate has not yet been issued.

Stratum estates

The Unit Titles Act 2010 allows titles to be issued for parts of buildings, for example an apartment or industrial park. The Act provides for a body corporate (comprising the unit owners) to be established, with a set of rules governing the use and maintenance of the building. The body corporate is tasked with insuring the building and controlling and maintaining the common areas. The unit owners pay a body corporate levy to cover its expenses. Before buying a unit, the vendor is required to provide to the purchaser a pre-contract disclosure statement setting out prescribed information relating to the body corporate, including information regarding body corporate levies. The information set out in the pre-contract disclosure statement will typically be provided by the body corporate secretary.

Barriers to buying land

In general, there are few restrictions on the purchase of land in New Zealand unless that land falls within one of the regulated categories under the Overseas Investment Act 2005.

For a detailed discussion of the screening regime, refer to the Overseas Investment Regime chapter. There are restrictions on the sale of land held by government agencies, which will need to be resolved before any sale to a private party (whether local or overseas) can proceed.

Māori land claims

Land claims by Māori, the indigenous people of New Zealand, are governed by the Treaty of Waitangi Act 1975. Under the Act, grievances are heard by the Waitangi Tribunal which can then make recommendations to the Government regarding the resolution of those grievances.

Recommendations for the return of land to Māori are generally applicable only in respect to land owned by the government or State-Owned Enterprises. Privately owned land is not subject to return to Māori ownership unless the title to the land has been specifically endorsed to that effect (and even then, current policy is not to exercise that right). If it was exercised, the current market value would be paid.

Minerals

Access and rights to prospect, explore and mine New Zealand's extensive petroleum and mineral estate, including coal, are governed by the Crown Minerals Amendment Act 2013 and Minerals and Petroleum Programmes issued under it.

All petroleum, gold, silver and uranium existing in land (including under the sea) is the property of the Crown (government). No person may prospect, explore for, or mine, government-owned minerals without an appropriate permit. Generally, a permit will be awarded to the person most likely to prospect, explore or develop the resource effectively and in accordance with the permit obligations and good practice.

Return to the Government is assured through a royalty regime, although there is provision in the Act for the Government also to participate in any given permit and thus derive a fair financial return through that avenue. The current policy is, however, not to exercise this right.

All transfers of or other dealings with a permit interest require the consent of New Zealand Petroleum and Minerals.

Chapter 15: Labour and Employment

Employment Relations Act

The Employment Relations Act 2000 (Act) is the principal statute governing employment in New Zealand. It aims to promote good faith in the employment relationship and the right of workers to bargain collectively.

Agreements must be in writing, and may be individual (between an individual employee and the employer) or collective (between one or more unions and one or more employer). Employers must hold a signed copy of employment agreements.

Union membership is not compulsory but all collective agreements must be negotiated and concluded by a union.

Good faith

The parties to an employment relationship must not do anything, either directly or indirectly, to mislead or deceive each other. They must be "active and constructive," as well as "responsive and communicative" in their dealings.

The Act also requires parties to bargain in good faith. Employers and employees/unions must, at a minimum, come to the bargaining table, listen and respond to what the other party puts forward. Parties bargaining for a collective agreement must conclude the collective contracts unless there are "genuine reasons" not to.

Employers proposing to take an action that may have an "adverse effect" on their employees must (subject to genuine although strict confidentiality exceptions) provide information about the decision and consult with their employees in good faith before the decision is made.

Sale of a business/contracting out

When engaging in a sale, merger or contracting out arrangement, as well as complying with the good faith/consultation requirements described above, an employer must negotiate with the proposed purchaser/new employer in relation to the employees. Such negotiations must include discussion about who will be offered employment with the new employer, and on what terms and conditions.

The Act also provides that "vulnerable employees" (primarily cleaning and food catering workers) are entitled to transfer to the new employer as of right and to bargain for redundancy payments with the new employer if their services are not required.

Termination

Most individual employment agreements are indefinite (i.e. they continue until terminated) but the law also recognises casual and fixed term employment arrangements. Fixed term agreements are lawful, but subject to certain restrictions.

The employee can end an indefinite employment arrangement by giving the specified notice period. However, an employer can terminate an employee's employment only after following a prescribed legal process and only for reasons of redundancy, misconduct, poor performance or incapacity. The parties can agree on a written 90-day trial period, during which the employer can end the employment arrangement without following the normal process or facing a personal grievance. There are strict requirements regarding trial period clauses (for example, agreements with trial clauses must be signed before the employee starts work).

There is no statutory right to redundancy compensation in New Zealand and, other than in very limited circumstances, compensation is only payable if it is provided for in the employment agreement.

Dispute resolution

The Act encourages mediation as the primary means of settling employment disputes. If mediation is unsuccessful, the parties may have their dispute decided by the Employment Relations Authority, an investigative body. If still unsatisfied, parties have a right of appeal to the Employment Court.

Very often, employment disputes are solved in mediation and do not proceed to litigation.

Strikes and lockouts

The only lawful strikes or lockouts are those which relate either to bargaining for a collective agreement or to health and safety issues. When a strike occurs, an employer can only use existing employees to perform the work of the striking employees, and then only if the existing employees agree to perform the work. External workers may only be employed when the work is necessary for public health and safety reasons.

Union access

Union representatives have a right to request access to a work place at reasonable times, in a reasonable manner, for purposes related to union business (which include recruiting members). Employers cannot unreasonably refuse access.

Working conditions

1. Workforce
In general, the New Zealand workforce is well-educated and well-trained. There are occasional shortages of senior management and skilled technical employees.

2. Wages
The minimum wage under the Minimum Wage Act 1983 is reviewed annually. Currently, the minimum wage for employees over the age of 16 is NZ$13.75 an hour or NZ$110.00 for an eight-hour day, or NZ$550.00 for a 40-hour week. Average total weekly earnings (full time equivalent) as at March 2013 were NZ$1031.00. (Source: Quarterly Employment Survey, Statistics New Zealand).

3. Holidays and leave

In addition to 11 statutory holidays, employees are entitled under law to at least four weeks' paid annual leave after 12 months of employment. After six months' continuous employment, employees are entitled to:
1. A minimum of five days' sick leave which they can also draw on when their spouse or someone who depends on them for care is sick or injured. Accumulated sick leave to at least 15 days must be carried over from year to year.

2. Bereavement leave of three days on the death of an immediate family member and of one day in all other circumstances where the employer accepts that the employee has suffered bereavement.

KiwiSaver

All new employees must be automatically enrolled in the KiwiSaver superannuation scheme. Automatic enrolment does not apply to temporary employees or to most business sale situations. Existing employees can also enrol in KiwiSaver if they wish.

Employees who are automatically enrolled have a six week period in which they can opt out. Employees who are members of KiwiSaver will have part of their gross earnings (minimum of 3%) deducted and paid by their employer to a superannuation scheme. Required employer contributions are also 3%. Total remuneration approaches (where employer contributions are deducted from the employee's salary) to KiwiSaver are generally permitted.

Payroll tax

Employers in New Zealand are required to deduct "Pay As You Earn" payroll tax (PAYE). Deductions are made on a fortnightly or monthly basis. The Inland Revenue Department may also require other deductions such as payments towards student loans or child support.

Parental leave

The Parental Leave and Employment Protection Act 1987 provides for both parents to take specified periods of parental leave (unpaid) on the birth or adoption of a child.

Government-funded paid parental leave

Primary caregivers are entitled to receive up to 14 weeks' paid leave of a maximum of $488.17(gross) per week, or 100% of the parent's previous weekly earnings, whichever is the lower.

To be eligible, parents must have been in paid employment with the same employer for at least an average of 10 hours per week for at least six months before the birth or adoption of a child.

The scheme allows the mother of the child to claim the paid leave or transfer the payment to the child's other parent, whether the father or a same sex partner.

Equal opportunities

Legislation is in place to ensure that employers cannot discriminate on the basis of an employee's (or prospective employee's) sex, marital status, religious beliefs, ethical beliefs, colour, race, ethnic or national origin, disability, age, political opinion, employment status, family status, sexual orientation or union involvement.

Accident compensation

In New Zealand, legal claims relating to personal injury are prohibited under the Accident Compensation Act 2001. Instead, the Act provides a statutory no-fault scheme under which cover is available for those suffering personal injury.

Coverage is broad based and includes most personal physical injuries, regardless of whether they occur in the workplace or elsewhere. Unless a crime is involved, pure mental injury is not covered by the scheme.

Compensation for injuries can take the form of payments for loss of earnings, health care treatment, cost of rehabilitation, independence allowance for disability, funeral expenses and death benefits for dependents. The scheme is funded from a number of sources, including levies on employers (linked to the amount of wages paid, with levy rates being determined on the basis of injury rates in the relevant industry), levies on employees, taxes on vehicle registration and taxes on petrol.

Accident compensation benefits are available to non-residents who are injured while in New Zealand. However, earnings-related compensation is not available to non-residents who derive their income from outside New Zealand.

Chapter 16: Intellectual Property

New Zealand's intellectual property laws are derived historically from English legislation and common law but have been influenced and reformed in recent years pursuant to the TRIPS Agreement and New Zealand's World Trade Organisation obligations.

Copyright

The Copyright Act grants exclusive rights to:
1. Copy a work (including, in relation to some works, storing the work in any medium by any means).
2. Issue copies of the work to the public.
3. Play, perform or show certain works in public.
4. "Communicate" the work.
5. Make an adaptation of the work.
6. Authorise another party to do any of the above.

Works that can be subject to copyright include:
1. Literary works (including computer programmes).
2. Dramatic works.
3. Artistic works (which may include drawings, moulds, dyes etc for utilitarian items such as machinery or clothing)
4. Musical works.
5. Sound recordings.
6. Films and broadcasts, including over the Internet.

To qualify for protection, a work must be "original".

In accordance with the Berne Convention (to which New Zealand is a signatory) copyright is established as soon as the work is created. A work does not need to be registered to gain protection.

The copyright in literary, dramatic, musical and artistic works generally lasts for the life of the author plus 50 years. Unlike in some countries, there is no bar in New Zealand copyright law against protection for industrially applied artistic works. However, the copyright term for industrially applied three-dimensional works is usually 16 years. Protection for industrially applied "works of artistic craftsmanship" lasts for 25 years. For other works, copyright generally lasts for 50 years.

Public performances of various kinds may also be the subject of separate protection given in certain circumstances to performers (but not in the performance of sporting activities). In addition, the Copyright Act protects "moral rights" which, (depending on the circumstances) may include:
1. A right to be identified as the author.
2. A right to object to derogatory treatment of a work.
3. A right against being falsely attributed as the author of a work.

Under New Zealand law, moral rights are not assignable. They can, however, be waived.

Patents

The Patents Act 2013 brings New Zealand generally into line with its major trading partners. The new Act will come into force once regulations are passed, possibly mid-2014.

The grant of a patent allows the owner to prevent others from exploiting (e.g. by making, using or selling) a patented invention for 20 years from the date of the patent.

An exception allows for third parties to do things "reasonably related" to the development and submission of information required under New Zealand law, or the law of another country, regulating the exploitation of the product.

A patent will be granted where the Commissioner of Patents is satisfied "on the balance of probabilities" that the application meets the requirements under the legislation. The most important of these are that the invention meets a universal or absolute novelty test and involves an inventive step (is not "obvious").

Certain things are excluded from patentability, including methods of medical treatment of human beings by surgery or therapy, a method of diagnosis practised on human beings, and inventions the commercial exploitation of which would be contrary to public order or morality.

"Embedded software" may be patented. "Swiss-type" patent claims in the pharmaceutical area will remain possible.

Various procedures are open to third parties wishing to object to or oppose a patent, both before and after grant. These include asking for a re-examination.

Registered designs

New and original industrial designs are registrable under the Designs Act 1953 if their shape, configuration, pattern, or ornamentation has visual appeal. However, because the Copyright Act protects industrially applied artistic works and useful articles in New Zealand, some businesses are content to rely on the protection given by copyright law only (although there are advantages to gaining registered protection under the Designs Act).

Under the Designs Act, the period of protection is for an initial five years, with rights of renewal for two further five-year periods.

Trademarks

Trademarks may be registered under the Trademarks Act 2002 (for goods and services). Once a trademark is registered, the proprietor has the exclusive right to use the trademark in relation to the goods and/or services for which it was registered.

The Act permits comparative advertising involving registered trademarks, except where the advertisements are "unfair" to the reputation of the mark. The Act also contains "anti-dilution" provisions to prevent unfair use of well-known registered marks in relation to goods and services which are dissimilar to those for which the mark is registered. Marks involving Māori language or symbols must be referred to a special committee for consideration before they are eligible for registration.

The Madrid Protocol allows for a multi-country trade mark application process.

Company names

A company name will not be approved if it is identical (or nearly identical) to an existing company name. Registering a company or reserving a company name gives no right to use the name as a trade mark, and provides no defence to infringement of third party trade mark rights. This is also the case in respect of domain names.

Unlike Australia, there is no register of business names in New Zealand.

Domain names

Regional domain names, such as ".co.nz" and ".govt.nz", are registrable in New Zealand. New Zealand courts have protected businesses against "cyber squatting" in some instances. In so doing, they have relied on principles developed in English and United States courts. There is also now a dispute resolution service operated by the Domain Name Commission, similar to the UK Nominet service.

Passing off

The law of passing off may also be invoked to protect business goodwill and is frequently used for the protection of trade marks (whether or not registered), names, logos, packaging designs and shapes. The principles are similar to those that have been developed in English and Australian common law.

Parallel importation

Importers can import lawfully made goods from foreign countries in commercial quantities without infringing the copyright of the "official" distributor in New Zealand, or of the overseas manufacturer. However, the prohibition against importing pirated goods, which were not made with the copyright owner's consent, remains in force.

The parallel importation of films is restricted for a period of up to nine months after their initial international release.

Confidential information

New Zealand law protects confidential information relating to trade secrets, such as business methods and industrial processes. As with passing off, the principles are similar to those that have been developed in English and Australian law. Non-disclosure agreements (NDAs) are useful for providing contractual rights to prevent disclosure of confidential information and can be used to supplement common law rights.

Chapter 17: Dispute Resolution

The structure of New Zealand's courts

The District Court is the court of first instance for most criminal prosecutions and civil cases. In criminal cases, whether the District Court has jurisdiction often depends upon the nature and seriousness of the alleged offence. In civil cases, the District Court will have jurisdiction if the amount in dispute is $200,000 or less. Above that amount, the claim must be advanced in the High Court. The High Court also has exclusive jurisdiction in certain matters as directed by statute, e.g. under the Companies Act 1993.

A judgment of a first instance court may be appealed. There is generally one right of appeal from the District Court to the High Court or from the High Court to the Court of Appeal. Second appeals require the leave of either the court appealed from or the court appealed to. All appeals to the Supreme Court require the leave of that Court.

The Supreme Court does not entertain appeals for the sole purpose of error correction, and will generally not grant leave unless:
1. The appeal involves a matter of general or public importance.
2. A substantial miscarriage may have occurred, or may occur unless leave is granted or
3. The appeal involves a matter of general commercial significance.

The Court of Appeal is therefore the final appellate court for most cases.

Specialist Tribunals

Outside the hierarchy of general courts is a range of courts and tribunals with limited jurisdiction or, more commonly, jurisdiction over specialist subject-matter. The specialist courts and tribunals include:

1. The Employment Relations Authority and the Employment Court, which have exclusive jurisdiction in respect of disputes arising out of the employment relationship.
2. The Environment Court, which has civil and criminal jurisdiction in relation to environmental matters, under the Resource Management Act 1991.
3. The Taxation Review Authority, which has jurisdiction to resolve certain disputes between the Commissioner of Inland Revenue and taxpayers, and
4. The Weathertight Homes Tribunal, which has jurisdiction to adjudicate on claims by owners of private property who believe that their residences have been damaged as a consequence of leaky building syndrome.

The decisions of the specialist tribunals may be appealed to, or reviewed by, the generalist courts. The Court having jurisdiction to hear the appeal is prescribed by statute. In some cases leave is required in order to appeal, and some appeals are restricted to questions of law.

Criminal prosecutions

With the exception of contempt of Parliament and contempt of Court, all criminal offences in New Zealand are prescribed by statute. The sentencing options available in respect of each statutory offence are also prescribed by legislation (usually the same statute as that which creates the offence in conjunction with the Sentencing Act 2002).

Although many offences may be prosecuted by individuals (referred to as "private prosecutions"), in practice offences are prosecuted by the Crown Solicitor or by the government department or institution having responsibility for the statute which is alleged to have been breached.

In New Zealand, Prosecution Guidelines do not permit a prosecutor to initiate or to invite a "plea bargain" in any criminal proceeding. However, it is permissible for a defendant to propose an arrangement whereby the defendant will enter a guilty plea either to some existing or amended charges, on the basis that other charges will be withdrawn or amended.

Rights and obligations imposed on litigants

Individuals are entitled to represent themselves before any court or tribunal, although most choose to be represented by lawyers. All lawyers authorised to practise in New Zealand have the right to appear in Court.

It is therefore unnecessary to instruct a lawyer practising solely as a barrister for appearances in Court. If a barrister is instructed, regulations require that the instruction be via a solicitor; meaning that the litigant will require a lawyer authorised to practise as a barrister and solicitor to act, in addition to the barrister sole.

In contrast to individuals, bodies corporate must ordinarily be represented by a lawyer. Only in exceptional circumstances will the generalist courts permit an unqualified representative (for example, a director) to appear on behalf of a body corporate.

Disclosure of documents

In criminal proceedings, the prosecution is required to disclose relevant documents to the defendant. There is no corresponding requirement on the defendant. In civil cases, each party is ordinarily required to disclose relevant documents to the other party or parties. Disclosure may be required on a general basis or in relation to specific issues only, but in either case each party must disclose both documents which support the party's case and documents which are adverse to it.

Certain documents are excluded from the disclosure requirement. The most commonly used exceptions are for communications between the party and his or her legal adviser and between the parties for the purpose of attempting to resolve the dispute. The existence of such documents must be disclosed, but ordinarily not the documents themselves.

Protections may also be sought for documents which are highly confidential or commercially sensitive. A common protection directed by the courts is for such documents to be disclosed to the other party's legal advisers and external experts, but not to the party himself or herself.

Court fees and costs awards

Fees are imposed for certain steps in civil proceedings and are usually payable by the party instigating that step. For example, the party commencing a proceeding must pay a filing fee (currently a maximum of $1,329.20 in the High Court). Similarly, the plaintiff must usually pay a fee for each hearing day after the first (currently $1,570.90 per half-day in the High Court).

In New Zealand, the generalist courts have an absolute discretion to award costs and disbursements to any party or parties to an application or proceeding. However, costs awards are ordinarily calculated on scales which are set out in the applicable Rules of Court. Costs awards calculated on this basis often equate to between 25% and 50% of the costs actually incurred by a litigant, with the result that a proportion of the costs incurred are irrecoverable. Disbursements (including the amount of fees charged by the Court) are usually recoverable in their entirety.

Alternative dispute resolution for civil disputes

Civil disputes are often resolved by negotiation directly between the parties or by mediation. Such resolution may occur at any time, whether before or after judgment in any proceeding, but most often resolution occurs before trial (or, in some cases, shortly after a trial has begun). The courts encourage resolution of disputes by the parties, and it is a requirement for many civil proceedings in the District Court that the parties first attend a judicial settlement conference before a trial is allocated.

Civil disputes may also be resolved by private arbitration, pursuant to the Arbitration Act 1996 (which is based on the Model Law on International Commercial Arbitration adopted by the United Nations Commission on International Trade Law). Some contracts provide for arbitration in the event of a dispute, but parties may also agree to arbitrate after a dispute has arisen.

New Zealand Legal Overview

1. In certain circumstances, some decisions of the District Court and the High Court may be reviewable by the High Court instead of being appealed.

2. A significant issue involving the Treaty of Waitangi is deemed to be a matter of general or public importance: s 13(3) of the Supreme Court Act 2003.

3. The ground of substantial miscarriage of justice is largely restricted to criminal proceedings. It would be rare for the Supreme Court to grant leave to appeal on this ground for a civil matter.

4. The Disputes Tribunal, for example, has limited jurisdiction to resolve some civil disputes involving amounts not exceeding $15,000 (or $20,000 with the agreement of all of the parties).

5. Appeals from the Employment Court are to the Court of Appeal. Appeals from the Environment Court and the Taxation Review.

6. Authority are to the High Court. Appeals from the Weathertight Homes Tribunal are to the District Court or the High Court depending upon the amount in issue.

7. For example, decisions of the Employment Court may be appealed to the Court of Appeal. However, such appeals first require the Court of Appeal to grant leave.

8. Appeals from the Employment Court and the Environment Court are restricted to questions of law, while appeals from the Taxation Review Authority and the Weathertight Homes Tribunal may be on questions of law and/or fact.

9. Such representation is permitted in most courts and tribunals, with the main exception being the Disputes Tribunal. Matters before the Disputes Tribunal tend not to be complex, and parties are generally not permitted to be represented by a lawyer.

10. Except in the Disputes Tribunal.

11. Costs awards are to reimburse the party in whose favour the award is made for legal fees incurred, and the award may not exceed the legal fees actually incurred by that party.

12. A judicial settlement conference (JSC) is a negotiation between the parties, facilitated by a judge and held in chambers. If a JSC does not result in a resolution between the parties, the judge who presided at the JSC is not permitted to preside at any subsequent trial, unless the parties consent or the only matter for resolution at trial is a question of law.

13. Such provisions are most common in agreements between commercial parties. There are some restrictions on imposing requirements to arbitrate in contracts between commercial parties and consumers (see, for example, s 11 of the Arbitration Act 1996).

Chapter 18: Accessing World Markets from New Zealand

New Zealand is a strong advocate for free trade and is signatory to a number of trade treaties.

China

New Zealand has a comprehensive free trade agreement (FTA) with the People's Republic of China, which came into force on 1 October 2008. One of the most important features is a phased reduction and elimination of tariffs on 96% of New Zealand's exports to China. The FTA contains rules to determine which goods qualify for tariff cuts and measures relating to customs procedures and cooperation, sanitary and phytosanitary provisions and technical barriers to trade. The Agreement also includes a comprehensive investment chapter, providing binding investor-state arbitration at the option of a qualifying investor.

Hong Kong

The New Zealand-Hong Kong, China Closer Economic Partnership (CEP) came into effect in 2011 and complements New Zealand's FTA with China by enhancing the potential for Hong Kong to be used as a platform for trade into Mainland China.

The CEP contains measures to improve business flows and promote cooperation in a broad range of economic areas of mutual interest, and is supported by legally-binding side agreements on labour and environment that are in line with New

Zealand's broader objectives for sustainable development. A legally-binding side agreement was also secured to negotiate an Investment Protocol within two years of entry into force.

Taiwan

ANZTEC - an Economic Cooperation Agreement with Taiwan was signed in July 2013 and will come into force in 2014. It provides for the immediate elimination of more than 70% of current tariffs on exports to Chinese Taipei, and for trade between the two signatories to eventually become tariff-free.

Australia

A set of trading agreements, known as CER, or Australia and New Zealand Closer Economic Relations, have been in place since 1983. These are now at a high level of maturity. Full free trade in goods was achieved in July 1990, four years ahead of schedule. Recent expansion of CER has included free trade in services, agreements to free up trade in areas such as aviation, and proposals to address taxation impediments to trade and investment. Both Governments are embarked on a programme of further reforms to increase harmonisation.

ASEAN

On 1 January 2010, New Zealand and Australia entered into a free trade agreement with the 10 member countries of the Association of South East Asian Nations (ASEAN), representing a market of over 500 million people. The FTA includes the eventual removal of tariffs on 99% of New Zealand's current exports to the four ASEAN markets of Indonesia, Malaysia, the Philippines and Vietnam.

Other agreements

New Zealand also has comprehensive free trade agreements in force with Singapore, Thailand, Malaysia and the 'P4' (New Zealand, Brunei, Singapore and Chile).

Agreements under negotiation

New Zealand is currently in negotiation with the US through the Trans Pacific Partnership (TPP) agreement to establish a free trade bloc. Other negotiating partners are Australia, Brunei, Canada, Chile, Malaysia, Mexico, Peru, Singapore, Vietnam and Japan.

New Zealand is also in FTA negotiations with India, South Korea, the Gulf Cooperation Council (GCC) and Russia-Belarus-Kazakhstan and is exploring with Japan the concept of entering an FTA with that country.

Chapter 19: Banking and Finance Sector

The Reserve Bank of New Zealand

The Reserve Bank of New Zealand is New Zealand's central bank. Its primary function is to formulate and implement monetary policy with the aim of achieving and maintaining price stability.

Policy targets are set to achieve this; these are currently defined as maintaining underlying inflation within a 1-3% range over the medium term, with a focus on keeping average inflation near 2%.

The Bank is required to publish a monetary policy statement every quarter.

The Reserve Bank's other functions are:

1. Maintaining the note and coin issue and the public debt and forex reserves.
2. Advising the Government on matters relating to monetary policy, banking credit and overseas exchange.
3. Licensing and the prudential supervision of banks and insurers.
4. Regulating non-bank deposit takers.

Financial institutions

Among the wide range of financial institutions in New Zealand are banks, building societies, private savings banks, merchant banks, finance companies, stock and station agents, trust and mortgage companies, small loan companies and insurance companies.

Banks

Following substantial de-regulation of the banking industry, New Zealand has maintained a relatively open policy on the entry of new registered banks with the philosophy that greater competition leads to greater efficiency and innovation.

There are currently 21 registered banks operating in New Zealand, representing a particularly high banks per capita figure by international standards. Not all of these banks operate full retail banking businesses.

The banks with the largest operations in New Zealand are:
1. ANZ National Bank Limited
2. ASB Bank Limited
3. Bank of New Zealand
4. Westpac (through Westpac New Zealand Limited and Westpac Banking Corporation), and
5. Kiwibank (which is owned by and run through New Zealand's postal operator, New Zealand Post).

Finance sector regulation

Any person who advises on financial products, provides an investment planning service in New Zealand makes investment management decisions on behalf of another person under an authority or receives, holds, pays or transfers client money is subject to disclosure requirements and conduct obligations under the Financial Advisers Act 2008 (FAA).

Persons providing services relating to more complex products will generally also have to become authorised by the Financial Markets Authority and meet qualification, training and competence requirements. Persons providing services on simpler products will generally need to be registered in New Zealand. The FAA applies regardless of the country in which the person performing the services resides.

The Financial Service Providers (Registration and Dispute Resolution) Act 2008 (FSPA) requires that any person or entity which provides a financial service is registered on the Financial Service Providers Register and (if they provide financial services to the public) is a member of a dispute resolution scheme. This includes financial advisers under the FAA, banks, securities issuers, KiwiSaver managers, custodians, money managers, credit contract providers, credit card providers, travellers cheque providers, currency exchanges, insurers, trustees, listed companies, and foreign exchange and futures dealers. Generally the FSPA will not apply to financial service providers who reside outside New Zealand and provide financial services in New Zealand.

Securities trustees and statutory supervisors are registered under the Securities Trustees and Statutory Supervisors Act 2011. Insurers are regulated by the Insurance (Prudential Supervision) Act 2010. The Financial Transactions Reporting Act sets out the current anti-money laundering regime, requiring financial institutions to carry out customer due diligence, identity verification and suspicious transaction reporting. An expanded regime, reflecting the FATF Recommendations will apply from 30 June 2013, under the Anti-Money Laundering and Countering Financing of Terrorism Act.

Financial markets

The New Zealand Exchange (NZX) regulates and facilitates New Zealand's three securities markets, as follows:

NZX Main Board

The NZX Main Board is New Zealand's principal market for equity securities. It features the securities of the majority of New

Zealand's listed companies and a number of overseas companies. There are approximately 170 companies listed on the NZX with a combined market capitalisation of approximately NZ$76.7 billion.

The NZX Main Board is suited to large and established enterprises. To list on the NZX Main Board the company must, among other things, have an appropriately qualified board of directors, at least 500 shareholders who hold at least 25% of the class of securities between them, and comply fully with NZX disclosure and other requirements. NZX also recommends that such companies have annual revenue of at least NZ$50 million. In certain situations, securities of overseas issuers which are listed on a recognised overseas stock exchange can be dual listed on the NZX without complying with a number of these requirements.

The NZX Main Board is the first of the world's markets to open each day, due to New Zealand's proximity to the International Date Line.

New Zealand Alternative Market

The NZX Alternative Market is designed for use by small to medium sized companies (with a minimum of 50 shareholders and recommended annual turnover of between NZ$5 million and NZ$50 million), which are fast-growing or looking for additional sources of capital.

The NZX Alternative Market is also suited to non-standard companies or entities such as co-operatives and mutual societies. It has a non-standard listing function that allows for closed trading for companies that have a defined group of shareholders. The NZX Alternative Market has lower levels of compliance and corporate governance, and lower listing costs than the NZX Main Board.

NZX Debt Market

The NZX Debt Market provides investors with a transparent and liquid market to buy and sell debt securities. Debt securities which may be offered on the NZX Debt Market include:
1. Government bonds.
2. State-Owned Enterprise bonds (bonds issued by companies owned by the Government and thus similar to government bonds but trading at slightly higher yields).
3. Local authority stock (issued by city councils and regional councils, etc).
4. Corporate bonds and debentures.
5. Money market instruments including treasury bills, bank bills, promissory notes and certificates of deposit.
6. Capital notes.
7. Perpetual notes, and
8. Preference shares.

Futures and options market

New Zealand futures and options contracts are currently traded on the Australian Securities Exchange (ASX), in relation to:
1. The NZX 15.
2. Share options in Contact Energy, Fletcher Building, Telecom and The Warehouse Group.
3. Electricity futures and options at the Otahuhu and Benmore grid reference points.
4. 90 day bank bills.
5. Three and 10-year government stock, and
6. 30-day official cash rate bonds.

Dealing in futures and options contracts requires authorisation from the Financial Markets Authority and compliance with the conduct and disclosure regime under the Financial Advisers Act 2008 and with the Financial Service Providers (Registration and Dispute Resolution) Act 2008.

Foreign exchange market

There are no restrictions on the buying and selling of foreign currencies. The New Zealand banking system offers a full range of foreign exchange services including spot, forward, futures, options and the more sophisticated derivative products.

Raising finance

New Zealand operates a very open regime. For businesses operating in New Zealand, there are no exchange controls, licensing, approval or similar regulatory restrictions.

Borrowers may raise finance on and off-shore and in the currency of choice. Banks are actively engaged in the provision of short and medium-to-long term debt to the consumer, commercial and corporate sectors. Market forces determine the level of interest rates.

Equity finance is available through issuing shares and listing on the NZSX or NZAX. Public offerings are regulated by the Securities Act 1978 and other securities legislation, and are generally made pursuant to a prospectus and an investment statement (although simplified disclosure can be made in certain circumstances).

Repatriation of funds

There are no restrictions on the repatriation of capital or earnings of a New Zealand business to overseas investors. This includes the remitting of dividends, profits, interest, royalties, management fees, etc. In many cases, however, non-resident withholding tax will be required to be deducted from the amount of those payments. For more information on New Zealand tax, please refer to the chapter on Taxation.

Chapter 20: Clothing and Footwear Sector in New Zealand

New Zealand is a world leader in the design and innovation of luxury natural fibres for use in the fashion industry, developing an industry now worth over $100million+GST at retail value.

New Zealand fashion designers have found international success due to their innovative and edgy designs. The use of natural fibres in fashion has helped gain exposure for New Zealand's research and development capabilities where merino wool has achieved worldwide acclaim.

Although the industry experienced growth of 7% from 2009-2010, the impact of the recession has led Textiles New Zealand to initiate change within the industry. An export growth strategy and better integration are significant elements of this.

Manufacturing is in decline due to cheaper production costs off-shore. Clothing manufacturers which remain in New Zealand are successful, innovative companies serving a niche market.

Textiles New Zealand is aiming to integrate the primary production and textiles manufacturing industries to add value to New Zealand's textile exports. UK and US are key market in this strategy which could lead to closer ties between the three countries and further joint opportunities.

The industry is not entirely market driven and this leads to the demise of some exporters. For market driven UK and American exporters, there are opportunities to fill this gap, although they should be aware of the differences between Australian and New Zealand tastes and climates which may affect sales.

Opportunities exist for US and UK exporters that serve niche and high-end markets.

The reduction of tariffs on clothing and footwear has meant that imported clothing and footwear is often cheaper than New Zealand made goods. Although tariffs have been reduced, a tariff of 10% still exists on clothing and footwear imports to New Zealand.

Due to the costs involved in manufacturing locally, some New Zealand designers are importing brands which complement their own ranges. This provides a low cost entry to market for US and UK designers. The opposing seasons also prove useful to US and UK companies who can export end of season goods to New Zealand where they will still be in season.

Chapter 21: Education and Training Sector in New Zealand

Similarities with UK cultural and education standards and the high regard with which UK products are held means that New Zealand educators and buyers are very willing to look at UK products and services.

The New Zealand education and training market is dynamic and provides opportunities for innovative US and UK products and services in a number of areas.

There is no intermediate layer between the Ministry of Education and schools themselves. Schools and tertiary institutions have considerable responsibility for their own governance and management, working within the framework of curriculum guidelines, requirements and funding arrangements set by central government and administered through its agencies.

Development of New Zealand's ICT infrastructure in education continues to be a priority for the New Zealand Government with technology increasingly key to education delivery.

The New Zealand Government has prioritised schools in its Ultra Fast Broadband (UFB) and Rural Broadband (RBI) initiatives, under which fibre is being rolled out across New Zealand to 97.7 percent of schools by June 2015. This will increase opportunities for online educational resource suppliers.

Teachers of religious studies and special needs report a lack of engaging resources. There are also opportunities for the provision of early childhood resources to support the recently implemented curriculum.

The New Zealand school curriculum is quite broad compared to that of the UK, with schools being able to deliver programmes relevant to their student's needs. Ministry of Education initiatives focus sector-wide on truancy, pastoral care, professional development, raising achievement, personalised learning and collaboration between agencies. This provides opportunities for US and UK companies in online programmes, software, books and other resources. New Zealand schools are responsible for seeking their own resources and online products are becoming extremely popular with New Zealand teachers.

The establishment of 8 trades academies in 2011 aimed at senior secondary students delivers trades and technology programmes based on partnerships between schools, tertiary and industry organisations. 2012 will see the commencement of a further 13 trades academies.

In the competitive corporate sector the importance placed on leadership management and growth is recognised in the plethora of courses available provided mainly from the private sector.

Opportunities also exist for change and empowerment training.

Chapter 22: Creative and Media Sector in New Zealand

Creative Industries are a growth sector for New Zealand. With one of the world's largest VFX post production facilities, New Zealand is gaining an international reputation for screen industry capabilities.

The Creative Sector has seen huge growth over the last decade, both in employment and revenue generation.

New Zealand has developed a global reputation for film and animation with post-production and VFX being key specialties. A number of tertiary institutions now offer digital media qualifications due to the growing reputation of New Zealand multimedia.

Advertising and Design in New Zealand has developed a reputation for keeping on top of trends, while adding a unique touch. This has led to many award winning ad campaigns for global companies.

There is a loyal following for British humour in New Zealand, with British programmes featuring significantly on television.

Screen industries: Companies have invested heavily in technology which allows for ease in remote working (eg. SohoNet). The reverse hemisphere seasons provide filming opportunities for US and UK companies and New Zealand has state of the art editing and VFX capabilities. New Zealand has a co-production agreement with the UK and if a project is structured appropriately may be eligible for Government funding.

Music: The British Council actively promotes British music in New Zealand. The sector is diverse including live performance, and a developing sound engineering industry. American music is well received in New Zealand.

Design: New Zealand designers in fashion and furniture concepts are gaining international recognition. New Zealand companies are receptive to British and American design and keen for interchange of ideas.

There are a number of organisations supporting the arts in New Zealand and these can provide guidance and opportunities. Creative NZ, NZ Film Commission and Designers Institute of NZ are examples.

When undertaking a project in New Zealand, the Employment Relations Act should be considered, and the NZ Film and Video Technician's Guild has drafted the Standard Policy for Work Conditions in the New Zealand Film Industry. Foreign cast and crew should be aware of their tax obligations while working in New Zealand.

Chapter 23: Franchising Sector in New Zealand

The franchising sector in New Zealand has doubled in size since 2003 (by number of units) as New Zealanders are highly aware of international brands and keen to adopt new ideas and technologies.

New Zealand has one of the highest rates of franchise systems per capita globally, with around 450 systems and 23,600 franchise units. Since the 1990s people are better informed about franchising and a good range of new, mature, local and international franchises have been established in New Zealand. Thirty-eight percent of franchise systems operate in service industries, representing over 50% of franchise units. Food and beverage franchises also do well in the market.

Mobile service franchises have found great success in New Zealand. Some areas of the mobile services sector, such as lawn mowing and gardening services now experience a lot of competition, but still see growth as these services become more popular. The limited overheads in this type of business model are advantageous to franchisees in such a geographically spread country as New Zealand.

Good food franchises do well in New Zealand. Local tastes need to be considered and the trend towards healthy eating is a key factor to consider.

Leisure and education franchises have experienced growth, with more room still for leisure and fitness franchises. New Zealanders like to keep active, with convenience and price being important factors in their choice of activities.

There is no specific legislation for franchises in New Zealand and they currently operate under the same commercial law as other businesses. The Health and Safety Act, Fair Trading Act, Employment Act and the Consumer Guarantees Act should be carefully considered.

The main growth strategies used by franchisors include offering exclusive territories, converting independents and encouraging multi-ownership for successful franchise operators.

Challenges noted by franchisors include the recruitment of franchisees, followed by the maintenance of standards and accessing franchisee capital.

Chapter 24: Petroleum and Minerals Sector In New Zealand

Exciting, underdeveloped and unexplored opportunities exist in New Zealand's petroleum and minerals industry, backed by a highly skilled and cost-competitive workforce.

Maui oil rig

Oil rig in the Maui field off Taranaki, North Island, New Zealand.

The petroleum and mineral sectors contribute around 2.5 percent annually to the New Zealand economy, but the country remains relatively under-explored. This potential is underpinned by high quality, publicly available prospective geology and a published geological research base.

The New Zealand Government is pragmatic and supportive toward investment in petroleum and minerals and welcomes responsible exploration. A key part of its business growth strategy is safe and environmentally responsible development of New Zealand's petroleum and mineral wealth.

The Government is committed to ensuring New Zealand has a robust and best practice regime that manages development every step of the way, delivers certainty for potential investors, and protects New Zealand's high environmental standards.

New Zealand's Exclusive Economic Zone (EEZ) covers about four million square kilometres and is the fourth largest in the world. Although exploration of the EEZ is at an early stage, potential for seafloor massive sulphides (SMS), titanomagnetite ironsands, ilmenite, phosphate nodules, manganese nodules and gold has been recognised. A 10-page overview has been published by the National Institute of Water and Atmospheric Research (NIWA) about New Zealand's EEZ potential resources.

New legislation governing the EEZ gives investors certainty about the regime that will apply in this huge marine environment.

According to GNS Science, New Zealand's leading provider of Earth, geoscience and isotope research and consultancy services, the Great South Basin offers huge oil and gas potential. The 360,000 square kilometres of remote, wild ocean south of New Zealand have been seismically quiet for 50 million years and there is a high chance petroleum has remained within trap structures. Oil majors Shell and OMV are already planning deep-sea exploration drilling in this area in 2014/15, with others also committing in other exploration areas.

Petroleum

There are multiple onshore and offshore sedimentary basins with known or potential hydrocarbon resources. The Taranaki Basin, covering an area of approximately 330,000 square kilometres and located off the west coast of the North Island, has been the only production basin in New Zealand to date, notably producing the global scale Maui oil and gas field in the mid-1970s, which continues production today. However, even Taranaki remains underexplored and considerable potential remains for further discoveries.

The rest of New Zealand's prospective areas are underexplored. However, a continued Government work programme to acquire seismic data for frontier basins is helping open up new areas of exploration, and in turn attract international interest and investment, assisted by a new system of exploration permit allocation.

Meanwhile, improving oil recovery technology is opening up smaller-scale onshore discoveries of commercial scale.

Gold

Compared to the complexity of its geology, mining history and the diversity of its mineral potential, New Zealand is underexplored. Gold has been New Zealand's most valuable mineral and has been produced continuously since the 1850s. Between 1860 and 1960, New Zealand produced more than 27 million ounces of gold. The country's gold output has increased strongly over the last 20 years, exceeding 430,000 ounces each year since 2008, a production level last achieved a century ago.

New Zealand's gold resource is produced commercially from two hard rock mines located in Waihi in the upper North Island and Macraes Flat in the South Island, as well as from a number of small and medium sized alluvial operations. The sector is experiencing buoyant conditions in New Zealand, with significant exploration activity.

Ironsand

Ironsand deposits located along 480 kilometres of coastline on the west coast of the North Island are among the largest known placer resources (shoal, or alluvial / sand deposit) in the world. These deposits are attracting growing international interest with increased permit activity and development plans in recent years.

The titanomagnetite ironsand placers occur in Quaternary beach and dune deposits and offshore marine deposits. Quaternary andesitic volcanic rocks of western Taranaki are the main source of the titanomagnetite, which has been concentrated by marine currents, wave and wind action.

Onshore resources have been estimated at about 1.3 billion tonnes of titanomagnetite. Geological modelling of source rocks suggests supply of about 39 billion tonnes of titanomagnetite into the offshore sedimentary environments. The cost of sea-mined titanomagnetite is expected to be low versus extraction by open-cast mining on land, making it potentially less vulnerable to swings in world steel prices.

Unconventional energy

Methane hydrates and coal bed methane are emerging energy resources in New Zealand. The country's undersea methane hydrates endowment is potentially one of the largest in the world, with the most commercially promising deposits, the Hikurangi Margin, covering around 50,000 square kilometres. Coal bed methane is thought to be contained in much of New Zealand's estimated 15 billion tonnes of coal resource.

Coal and lignite

Approximately five million tonnes of coal is mined annually in New Zealand, about half of which is bituminous coking coal. This world class resource is suitable for use in steel making due to its low ash and low sulphur levels, and is open-cast mined on the South Island's West Coast.

Other minerals

Silver, aggregate, limestone, high quality ceramic clay, dolomite, perlite, pumice, salt, serpentinite and zeolite are also produced in New Zealand for local and export markets. Additionally there are resources or potential for a wide range of other metallic and non-metallic minerals including platinum group metals, base metals (copper, titanium and tungsten), sulphur, phosphate and silica.

Chapter 25: Conclusion

New Zealand has an open-market economy, a stable political system, and has been recognised as one of the world's least-corrupt countries. This allows businesses to operate with confidence in New Zealand.

Exporters to New Zealand should be prepared to adapt their business model to suit the nation's small population and geographic isolation.

There is a constant demand for innovation in the local agricultural sector, the most important industry to New Zealand's economy.

Global market conditions: Economic uncertainty among New Zealand's trading partners could potentially limit the country's export trade through 2013/2014.

Small population: New Zealand's relatively small population can restrict consumer demand. Businesses have limited opportunities to leverage scale, and appropriately skilled workers may not be readily available.

Agriculture, Forestry and Fishing: Due to its environmental diversity, New Zealand supports a broad range of agricultural industries, producing large amounts of dairy, lamb, beef and wool.

Biotechnology: This has become a growth industry in New Zealand, largely due to the strength of the agricultural sector and the state-supported healthcare scheme. Demand from abroad for quality biotech products is increasing.

Creative: Following several high-profile film and television productions, New Zealand's creative sector is in a growth phase. Film, television, visual design and digital are becoming key creative subsectors.

Information and Communication: As the Asia Pacific region has developed; New Zealand's information technologies sector has seen increasing demand.

Food and Beverage: New Zealand's climate lends itself to producing a wide variety of foods and beverages. The industry encompasses companies of varying sizes from small microbreweries to multi-national dairy producers.

Australia and New Zealand have a very close and low-regulation economic relationship. The Australia-New Zealand Closer Economic Agreement (ANZCERTA) has been in place since 1983, and it represents one of the closest and most comprehensive trade agreements anywhere in the world. New Zealand is also part of free- trade agreements with the ASEAN, China, Hong Kong, Malaysia, Singapore, Thailand and several South Pacific countries.

There are certain restrictions that can be imposed by New Zealand's Overseas Investment Act 2005 on foreign investment. Whether or not these restrictions are exercised may vary on any trade agreements that apply.

The Overseas Investment Office may be required to authorise the acquisition of significant business assets that exceed $100 million in value. They also monitor fishing quotas and can authorise the attainment of sensitive land. These types of land include:
1.   Non-urban land of more than five hectares
2.   Offshore islands

3. Land adjacent to lakes and the foreshore
4. Land of conservational or historical significance.

New Zealand continues to lead the rankings for the Ease of Doing Business and for Starting a Business respectively.

Good Luck!!